The 10-Minute Retriever

The 10-Minute Retriever

How to Make an Obedient and Enthusiastic Gun Dog in 10 Minutes a Day

John L. Dahl

JOHN AND AMY DAHL

Amy Dahl

Willow Creek®
P R E S S

Minocqua, Wisconsin

Published by Willow Creek Press
P.O. Box 147, Minocqua, Wisconsin 54548
For information on other Willow Creek Press titles, call 1-800-850-9453

Cover design by Patricia Bickner Linder
Edited by Andrea K. Donner

Library of Congress Cataloging-in-Publication Data

Dahl, John I.
    The 10-minute retriever : how to make an obedient and enthusiastic gun dog
in 10 minutes a day / by John and Amy Dahl.
        p. cm.
    ISBN 1-57223-303-6 (softcover : alk. paper)
            1. Retrievers--Training. 2. Hunting dogs--Training. I. Title:
        Ten minute retriever. II. Dahl, Amy, 1962- III. Title.
    SF429.R4 D34 2001
    636.752'735--dc21
                                                                            2001000691

TABLE OF CONTENTS

ACKNOWLEDGEMENTS

We wish to thank the following people for their friendship and assistance through the years of training and trialing retrievers, as well as to recognize their excellence as trainers and competitors. There are, of course, many others whom we admire and from whom we have learned. Our past training partners and models in the retriever world include: Lanse Brown, Anton Dahl, Bach Doar, Mac and Lynne DuBose, Ed Forry, Delma Hazzard, Bill and Mary Hillmann, Christina Jones, Jane Kelso, Lawrence Martens, Pat Nolan, Mike Osteen, Roger Reopelle, Jay Sweezey, D.L. Walters, and Bob Willow. Special thanks to Bob Johnson, who got John started with retrievers.

We also wish to thank Steve Smith for his assistance and encouragement of our writing efforts.

INTRODUCTION

W̲E HAVE WRITTEN THIS BOOK to fill a need. While there are some excellent resources (books and videos) available on advanced topics, we are constantly asked for detailed information on the basics of retriever work: gaining control without sacrificing enthusiasm, force-fetching, forcing on back, and how to raise a puppy to be a gun dog or competitive prospect. These accomplishments and the overall training of a well-mannered, effective waterfowl dog are well within the ability of the average retriever owner, if he or she has the necessary guidance.

We have read a lot of books looking for the perfect reference. The "classics" in the field lack discussions of force-fetching and puppy work. Many retriever books treat obedience and force-fetching too briefly for owners of energetic or strong-willed dogs. Books on obedience advocate some things that are best avoided with retrievers, say nothing about developing drive, and are not tailored to the temperaments of the retrieving breeds. Many retriever books assume that all dogs respond exactly the same. Others disregard the body of knowledge that exists about retriever behavior and training, to invent new methods that are fundamentally flawed.

Hence this book. It is intended to be a resource that will enable the motivated retriever owner to train his or her dog, humanely and well. It is grounded in our knowledge as professional trainers of hunting and field-trial retrievers, using techniques passed down and improved upon by generations of trainers, refined under the intense competition of retriever field trials. It draws from our experience teaching owners to train their dogs, and from feedback we have received on training articles we have published. It is dedicated to all of the current, former, or future retriever owners who have the capacity to be moved by good dog work, and the desire to initiate their own dogs into the world of disciplined retrieving. We hope that with its aid you will be able to teach your dog to do all you desire, and we wish you good training.

CHAPTER 1

PRINCIPLES & EQUIPMENT

WE WOULD FIRST LIKE TO MAKE IT CLEAR that our intention is not to convey the idea that a retriever can be trained in ten minutes flat. Of course, that is obvious. We hope that anybody undertaking the task of producing a well-trained working retriever will be endowed with sufficient patience and energy to see the job through to a satisfactory level. Further, we hope that an aspiring retriever trainer will enter this project in a spirit of love for dogs, and will desire to continue training and improving upon the dog's performance throughout his life.

This book is not written for the lazy person. It is written for all of you who face limitations of time due to the necessity of providing for yourselves and your families, and who would like to achieve the remarkable result of a trained hunting or competition retriever. The dedicated but busy trainer can do this in short, approximately 10-minute, work sessions.

The figure of ten minutes is not arbitrary. Our experience indicates that a dog's interest level, and associated learning gains, begins to fall off sharply somewhere in the five- to ten-minute range. Professional trainers typically train from 15 to 25 dogs at a time. At the upper limit, it is possible to give 25 dogs a good workout twice a day and keep their level of proficiency improving. We allow, of course, for the fact that dogs, like people, have their ups and downs.

But how is it possible for a professional retriever trainer to give 25 dogs adequate training in an 8-hour day to keep them competitive in retrieving's toughest sport — field trials? Generally, once a test (or lesson) is set up, it is possible to train six dogs an hour. This schedule makes for a total of 24 dogs in the first four hours, and the same for the second four. Our point is not to argue that a pro can do a good job with a truck and trailer load of dogs, but to illustrate that the most skillful and proficient retrievers in the country are trained largely on a schedule of 10-minute sessions.

In most cases, during the first few months of training, much of the time spent will be in the convenience of your back yard. It does not take much space to teach basic obedience, force fetching, and the other rudiments; in fact, much of it can be done in your living room or kitchen. You can schedule ten-minute lessons at your convenience.

As your dog advances and you do more work in the field, your time investment will increase to encompass transportation, test setup, etc. You may join a training group in which you take your turn at throwing dummies or birds in order to get others to throw for your dog. While the actual training allotment may be approximately ten minutes, time taken getting equipment together, shooting the breeze with training partners and so forth, can run the training session into considerably more time.

How many of these ten-minute sessions per day or week are required? At least one per day with the possible exception of one day off per week. This is minimal. Your dog will probably not progress very well if he is not given at least this much attention.

How many of these sessions per day would optimize your training efforts?

We suggest that one morning and one evening session is close to ideal, with some periods of socialization, exercise, and other amenities in between. Some trainers really go at it tooth and nail with as many as four training sessions per day. Some of these individuals have accomplished remarkable things in a very short period of their dog's life, such as making FC or AFC titles before two years of age, or making Master Hunters at 12 or 13 months. These accomplishments are a testimony to the dog training expertise as well as the dedication of these trainers, and to the inherent excellence of their dogs.

In the case of average dogs, which most of us have, striving for extraordinary achievement is not advisable. Naturally, do not hold a great student back, but the more common pitfall with novice trainers is pushing too hard. Failing to cover the groundwork thoroughly, or worse, souring the dog toward work, commonly results.

Training dogs over a period of years has revealed that they have both short-term and long-term memories. Short-term learning may be accomplished in a few sessions, perhaps even one. The dog may come back the next day demonstrating that he remembers what he was taught the day before. However, if the training procedure is not repeated for a period of days or longer, he will probably demonstrate that he has forgotten that lesson. Most lessons, from obedience through force fetching on up, take several weeks to "set" in a dog's long-term memory.

We cannot over emphasize that these lessons should be limited to ten minutes, or even five, as a dog's attention, and his willingness to accept the pressure of training, will begin to flag at about that time. Training in excess of this will generally reverse the learning process, causing a dog to backslide and become reluctant and unenthusiastic.

The fine professional trainer Charlie Kostrewski said, "Never try to accomplish too much in one day — get a little done, apply a little pressure if you have to, and come back for more tomorrow. Don't rough the dog up too much, quit while he still has enthusiasm — and feel for the dog." We think this is still good advice.

The best modern trainers seem to subscribe to this thinking. In most cases, if a dog has difficulty with a test, particularly a marking test, these trainers will see him through as best they can by simplifying (as described in the text). After the correction, the dog is generally put up without repeating the test. The next day, the principle of that test is repeated in another location, looking for improvement.

We have found that repeating a principle over and over in various settings until that idea is well learned is preferable to "jumping around" by challenging your dog with a dizzying potpourri of tests. For example, if you want to teach an especially difficult triple mark, you may do it by running the three marks as singles on Monday and Tuesday, throwing the triple with dummies on Wednesday, doing the same test with dead birds on Thursday, and with two dead birds and a shot flier on Friday. Then you might be ready to run that difficult test in the Master Hunter or a devastating triple in the Amateur All-Age on Saturday.

Finally, we note that 10-minute sessions are good for the trainer's motivation as well as the dog's. Consistency of work (daily or twice-daily sessions) is critical to a dog's progress. Even procrastinators and people under time pressure can usually manage a ten-minute break with their dog once a day. The combination of surprisingly rapid progress with brief outings is reward enough for most beginners to become consistent, enthusiastic trainers. Just keep on training at least once every day — if you can't spare ten minutes, work for five, or review yesterday's lesson for one minute if that is all the time you have.

Principles

We have written this book for the purpose of helping you train your retriever humanely, effectively, and in a manner that is enjoyable to both of you. You will benefit most, however, if you recognize its inherent limitations by virtue of being a book.

One of the most important keys to humane and rapid training is the ability to "read" your dog; that is, to evaluate her responses to a training procedure. If the dog did what you expected, she may understand or she may have just been lucky. If she does something else, or nothing at all, she may be confused, recalcitrant, or you may have inadvertently taught her to do the wrong thing. Experience is the greatest aid in interpreting these responses and deciding how to proceed. That is exactly what we cannot put into a book. If we attempted to catalog all the possible responses to each training procedure, this book would be inordinately long. In places, we have described a few common responses, but you can expect your dog to do something completely different at some point.

It is easier to learn from a person than from a book, and one way to fill in the gaps is to seek help from an experienced trainer. Many pros will give lessons for a reasonable fee, and many amateur trainers will be more than willing to help if you throw some birds for their dogs. This solution has its pitfalls, though. Those most ready to offer advice may be least qualified to give it. Look for someone who obtains good results with a minimum of correction in the field, and avoid those who preach that it isn't a good training session unless the dog gets "burned" with the electric collar. Someone whose dogs are stylish and eager, but also under control, is likely to have the ability to help you interpret your dog's behavior.

If you choose to train on your own, we offer some simple guidelines for making training decisions. If your dog performs an exercise correctly, practice it a few times to give her the reward of competence. If your dog is nearly perfect in these repetitions, move on. Build on that exercise or introduce a new one. If failure at the new level shows your dog didn't really understand, no harm has been done. Simply fall back and review the previous exercise. On the other hand, holding a dog back may adversely affect her ability to learn.

If your dog does not perform as intended, you will almost never go wrong treating the problem as a lack of understanding. In basic obedience, a correction may be justified if your dog has previously demonstrated that she understands the exercise. In most other situations, the fastest and easiest solution is to simplify what you ask of her. If you back up to an exercise your dog knows well, you are justified in correcting a failure or refusal. Then progress to the current problem in a series of smaller steps. This may require one training session, or several.

In summary, any time you find yourself asking WHY a dog is doing something wrong, it is a good idea to assume that it is because the dog has not been thoroughly taught how to do it right. Plan some sessions to teach correct behavior step by step instead of resorting to a correction which your dog may not understand.

Training Methods

There are many ways to train dogs. We do not train any two dogs exactly the same. In this book, we present an approach that has been successful for a wide variety of dogs. Our techniques are based on methods developed by some of the nation's best retriever trainers over decades of training and competition, plus a few of our own invention. They have been tested time and again, in competition and hunting, and they work.

More important than the precise method, however, is the progression of training. Build upon earlier exercises and make sure the fundamentals of *sit, here, heel,* and *fetch* are solid before attempting advanced work, and always consider how a day's lesson will affect your dog's attitude. We caution you to make sure all of your training is presented to your dog in a consistent fashion. Mixing fundamentally different approaches may be confusing to your dog, and rob her of confidence. Following our method throughout, while not the only way to train a dog, is a good way to avoid confusion.

Training Principles: Behavior and Behaviorism

Any action performed by a dog is *behavior,* from scratching itself to executing a complicated retrieve. *Behaviorism,* the scientific study of behavior founded by B. F. Skinner, has elucidated principles as to how behavior is influenced and controlled. While these principles do not rely on thought or conscious learning, it is worth noting that they do not necessarily imply the absence of a thinking process. In fact, the principles of behaviorism may be applied productively to human subjects as well as to dogs. Although our training techniques were developed by experimentation and trial and error, they constitute a highly-effective application of the principles of behaviorism.

We include this section not in an attempt to invent a new training method starting from the principles of behaviorism — we don't believe we could surpass the methods developed by trial-and-error over several decades — but to provide a structured basis for some of our recommendations. The need for consistency in training, the futility of punishment, the importance of developing a puppy's love of retrieving to the highest order possible, and other important training practices, can all be explained in terms of the principles of behaviorism.

Reinforcement, i.e. Reward

Psychologists tell us that animals and humans learn faster, and retain lessons better, when correct responses are rewarded or "positively" reinforced, than when learning is motivated only through punishment. In retriever training, most of the rewards are built into the work. Most retriever trainers do not characterize their work in terms of rewards, yet today's highly-refined training methods manipulate reinforcement very effectively.

As discussed in Chapter 3, the principal reward in retriever training is the *act of retrieving*. Therefore, puppy training needs to emphasize the development of a dog's love of retrieving in order to make that reinforcement as strong as possible to support later training. Other rewards dogs quickly learn to like are praise (discussed in Chapter 4) and the satisfaction of completing an exercise that has been learned (making repetition a useful motivator). Most dogs also seem to enjoy movement: walking briskly, running, jumping, etc.

Correction

Some behaviors, such as chewing, digging, and running away while being chased, are inherently rewarding to most retrievers. These are called *self-reinforcing behaviors*. The more a dog is allowed to indulge in them, the greater its motivation to repeat them. Chasing a moving object and carrying something in the mouth (the behaviors we modify into retrieving) are self-reinforcing to most retrievers.

Other behaviors are likely to be "accidentally" reinforced in the normal course of events if we do not interfere. Jumping up on people is reinforced by closeness to the person's face, and often by attention. "Cheating" (taking a roundabout route on a retrieve) may be rewarded by speedy completion of the retrieve. We address these unwanted activities, whether they are spontaneous or occur in training, by preventing reinforcement. With little puppies, we simply prevent opportunities for the behavior.

Once a dog begins her training, we can use correction to teach her not to engage in unwanted behavior.

The point of correction is to remove the reinforcement for undesirable behavior, replacing it with a deterrent. A correction interrupts a dog's action before it can be completed, and is usually unpleasant for the dog. For example, in the case of a dog jumping up on people, the owner could make sure the dog is wearing her training collar with leash attached when guests come to the door — then give a solid two-handed jerk on the leash, sideways and down, when the dog is in mid-jump.

Corrections for unwanted behavior must be applied consistently in order to be effective. Withholding the correction allows the action to be reinforced. Behavioral science has found that part-time reward (or "variable-ratio schedules of reinforcement") is even more effective at intensifying behavior than is constant reward.

A correction should be just forceful enough to convey that the dog's action is "not an option." If the action is promptly repeated, the correction was ineffective. Beyond the point of effectiveness, however, there is no benefit to additional harshness.

Punishment

Many dog trainers use the term "punishment" for unpleasant consequences that follow an infraction. Because its timing allows the behavior to be completed and reinforced, punishment is ineffective, even if quite harsh. It is likely to lead to problems such as apprehensiveness and lack of confidence, so we recommend you avoid it.

Pressure

Pressure in retriever training may mean different things. It refers to the discomfort we inflict in force fetching and forcing on back to condition dogs to pick up a dummy on command and to go when sent. In these applications, *pressure* corresponds to what the behaviorists term "negative reinforcement," a conditioning procedure where the dog's execution of a desired action results in the cessation of an unpleasant stimulus.

The term *pressure* is also used for the stress of training. This includes the burden of awareness that a certain action is desired, and possible confusion as to what that action is. Difficulty of tests, harshness of conditions, frequency of corrections, and length of training sessions all contribute to this stress. Dogs vary in their degree of "toughness" under training pressure, and many benefit from the trainer's attention to minimizing it. Our approach to training is tailored to limiting pressure — starting with our advice to keep training sessions short.

Distractions and Proofing

Your dog's attention may be distracted by many things: other dogs, cats, people, smells, new places, etc. For ease of learning, most lessons should be introduced in a familiar setting with as few distractions as possible. Exercises learned in this setting, however, will appear to be forgotten as soon as your dog is distracted. To make your dog's training useful in daily life, the basic obedience commands must be "proofed," or practiced in the presence of increasing distractions.

Training Principles Checklist

1. Keep sessions short.
2. Give your dog a break: treat failures as lack of understanding, especially in retrieving.
3. Be consistent in and outside of training sessions. Use the same command every time, and be careful never to encourage behavior (bad habits) you are trying to eliminate.
4. Pay attention to timing, especially of corrections.
5. Use a release command to give a definite end to commands

such as "heel" and "stay." The release command is discussed in detail in Chapter 4.

6. Be definite. Act confident and authoritative, never tentative. Planning training sessions to minimize the unexpected will help.

7. Don't train when you are angry or upset, and don't take it personally when your dog does not perform as intended.

8. Keep progressing. When your dog is competent at one level, move on.

9. No matter how much effort you put into setting up a test for your dog, if she demonstrates that she is inadequately prepared in some way, forget the test and work on whatever fundamentals the dog needs.

10. Do not use more force/correction than the minimum needed to get the job done.

Things to Consider Throughout Training

Most retriever training consists of building up a dog's repertoire, step by step. A few crucial concepts, however, require constant attention. A dog's attitude toward retrieving and training is a product of her entire training program, and choices should always be made with this in mind. Attitude toward water is a separate issue. When training in and around water, be aware that any correction, confusion, or other stress applied while your dog is in the water may potentially lead to fear of the water. We recommend that you train only in warm water, 56° or above (hunting is different), and plan your rate of progress so that training sessions will go as smoothly as possible.

Certain potential bad habits must be anticipated and prevented. Cheating (running around water or obstacles), creeping (moving out in front of the handler when birds are thrown), and mishandling birds are easy to prevent, but often difficult or impossible to cure.

Training Aids/Equipment

We recommend making use of a variety of equipment throughout this book. We describe most of the items here to avoid having to do so repeatedly in the chapters on training.

Choke Collar

The basic collar is the chain training collar, or "choke chain." It is used with a lead or check cord to make jerk-and-release corrections, and is not designed to be held tightly in a choking fashion. There is a right and a wrong way to put it on — only the right arrangement allows it to release after a correction. The "running end" to which the lead is attached, passes through the other ring and over the top of your dog's neck when she is in position beside you. The picture shows the proper configuration for a dog that works from your left. The choke chain should not be loose. We recommend the smallest size that will slip over your dog's head.

The choke collar works best if your dog is not wearing any other collar. We recommend taking the choke collar off when you are not actively supervising your dog because of the danger of its getting caught on something and causing injury.

Pinch Collar

The pinch collar looks fearsome but is an excellent training device. Many retrievers are physically insensitive and do not respond well to standard corrections with the choke collar. Rather than jerking with all your might on the choke collar, if you do not get quick results, try the pinch collar. Strenuous yanking may cause injury to your dog's neck, and it can also put the trainer out of sorts and lead to an adversarial training relationship.

Because of reports that pinch collars can separate, we recom-

Proper arrangement and fit of choke collar for a dog that heels on the left.

mend using them together with a choke collar. By adding or removing links, adjust the pinch collar to ride high on your dog's neck behind her head. The looser chain collar should lie lower on your dog's neck. Attach the lead to the rings of both collars. Should the pinch collar separate, your dog can still be controlled by the leash attached to the choke collar. Do not leave the pinch collar on your dog when you are not training.

Training Stick

The training stick is usually 30"-40" long and can be anything from a riding whip to a broom handle. A flexible switch is least likely to cause accidental injury. If you use a hard stick, be extremely careful not to strike your dog's spine, legs, or other bony areas. The stick has a variety of uses. It can be used as a guide to aid in teaching heeling and returning to heel, as a distraction in the stick-fetch routine, and to apply pressure in forcing on back.

Leads

A leather leash is necessary if you will be making use of jerk corrections with the choke or pinch collars. Leather is much easier on the hands than nylon, cotton, or rope. Six feet is a good length for training, permitting you to control the amount of slack you give your dog.

Check Cords

Check cords of varying lengths can be made with a bolt snap and braided polypropylene. The polypropylene floats, resists rotting, and never tangles if coiled up figure-eight style after use. It will not fray, either, if you melt the strands together over a flame at each end. To attach a bolt snap, form the melted end into a point with wet fingers. Feed the point through the eye of the snap, loosen the braid about 6" from the end, and feed the pointed end down the center of the loosened section.

Electric Collar

Much has been said and written about the electric collar as a training aid — mostly by people who have never used one, or taken the time to learn to use one correctly. It is a device which allows you to push a button and shock your dog, even at great distances. Modern collars allow for fine control of the intensity of shock.

The potential for abuse of the electric collar is significant. It enables a hot-tempered trainer to hurt a dog with little effort or forethought. Our addiction to push-button control may mislead us to think we can control the dog with the transmitter. We can't; we can only shock the dog. Shock does not teach, explain, or resolve confusion. The "e-collar" can be a useful training tool as part of a well-conceived, step-by-step training program. It is not useful as a shortcut or a cure for our training mistakes, or a last-ditch attempt to stop a dog that has gone out of control. If a dog does not understand what her handler wants, shocking will only make her fearful and tentative.

Keeping these limitations in mind, the e-collar has advantages not available with any other training device. It can deliver well-timed correction at a distance with no danger to the dog. Since one well-timed correction is often more effective than a dozen delayed, harsher ones, the e-collar makes possible safer, less-stressful training. In most cases, a small number of corrections on carefully-planned setups are sufficient to keep a dog minding her P's and Q's, even at distances of hundreds of yards.

The electric collar is also a great advantage in obedience and yard work with most dogs. Some dogs anticipate corrections in a manner that impedes training. It is difficult to administer effec-

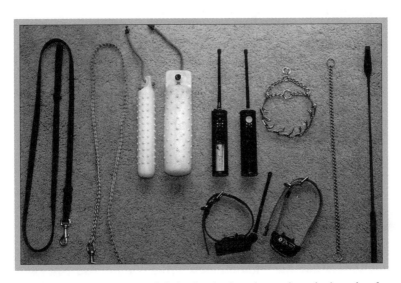

Training equipment. From left: leather leash, polypropylene check cord, soft plastic retrieving dummies, two designs of electric collar with transmitters, pinch collar, choke collar, training stick.

tive leash or stick corrections when a dog can anticipate them. It can be a struggle to overcome these problems by conventional means. The electric collar gives the trainer a means of correction that is not heralded by arm or stick movement, enabling problems with anticipation to be smoothly resolved.

Reliability is the most important consideration in choosing an electric collar. A collar that fails to deliver shock on demand can allow a dog to succeed in committing the infraction a training session was designed to discourage. Much careful work may be undone—and harsher treatment will likely be required to regain control. We have tried most of the brands of electric training collars. The Tri-Tronics brand collars have consistently stood out for their reliability and appropriate design for retriever work.

Differences in Dogs

Many challenges in dog training arise from individual differences in dogs. We have seen tremendous ranges in every physical and temperament trait that bears upon a dog's ability to learn and upon her effectiveness in the field. A few of these traits are: tractability, intelligence, sensitivity to cold or rough going, desire to retrieve, ambition, training toughness (ability to respond to training enthusiastically, and take corrections in stride), natural inclination to mark, to line, and to cast, sensitivity of nose and ability to use it wisely, and enthusiasm for birds. In the true stories about dogs we have owned and trained that follow each chapter, we have tried to illustrate the uniqueness of individuals, and the need for creativity to work with each dog's particular strengths and weaknesses.

As you and your dog progress with training, you will get a feeling for the areas that are stumbling blocks, and those she seems to take to naturally. Try not to bemoan your dog's shortcomings. Many field champions and great hunting dogs have had significant flaws. Instead, capitalize on your dog's strengths to help compensate for those areas in which she does not excel — and enjoy what she has to offer, instead of comparing her to your buddy's dog or your old dog. No two dogs are alike. Just train your dog as you find her, and deal with problems as they occur.

While there are distinct differences among average individuals from the different retriever breeds, we feel that trying to characterize the different breeds here would do more harm than good. It can be hard enough to evaluate a dog's temperament and response without the added confusion of establishing a breed stereotype.

The techniques we describe are well-suited to all retriever breeds. They have been refined through application to hundreds of Labradors and Chesapeakes, dozens of golden retrievers, and a smattering of flat-coats, tollers, and other sporting breeds (and one pit bull). In fact, despite the Lab's reputation for resilience in training, we believe the majority of Labradors, as well as the other breeds, benefit from an emphasis on clarity, step-by-step progression, and constant attention to attitude.

Personality Types

A few "types" deserve mention. The first could be called "skeptical." Many Chesapeakes are of this nature. The skeptical dog does not accept anything the first time it is presented. This dog is likely to "test" the trainer's commitment to making her perform each command, each step of the way. We think it is constructive to think of these dogs not as lacking cooperation, but as wanting to make absolutely sure that you "mean it" when you give a command. They may require more repetition in training, but there is usually a payoff in that they often retain what they have learned better than some who are quicker to comply.

Some of the skeptical dogs are also "soft." The soft dog is apt to take correction and/or pressure "personally," acting put-upon and dejected. These dogs must be trained carefully, sometimes requiring pressure to be applied less frequently than with most dogs. Soft dogs may be sensitive and resentful if they are mistakenly corrected while they are trying to comply with a command. Softness can occur in any breed, but is common in Chesapeakes and goldens, especially the bitches.

In contrast to the soft dogs which tend to take things personally, some dogs are essentially phlegmatic. They are perfectly agreeable, but may seem unresponsive in early obedience training, appearing downright hard-headed. Often the problem is simply that the corrections used are too light to make an impression. Switching from a choke collar to a pinch collar, and making sure corrections are definite and emphatic, can bring about sudden improvement. Dogs of this nature generally do not resent training and are resilient in the face of occasional training mistakes. Many Labs are phlegmatic in their response to training, but this type of response is also common in goldens and occurs in a fair number of Chesapeakes.

A small minority of dogs are contrary. They begin training with an apparent dedication to thwarting the trainer's intentions at every turn. These dogs do things such as lie on their backs when the trainer tries to make them sit — not out of submissiveness, but because it is nearly impossible to wrestle them into a "sit" from that position. Unlike the phlegmatic dogs, they do not undergo a sudden transformation when a more effective means of correction is applied — they are more likely to comply with the immediate demand, and invent a new way to confound the trainer on the next exercise. Contrary dogs tend to be very aware of training aids, and to become "collar-wise" even when the e-collar is introduced and used properly.

These dogs are a challenge to train! Frequently they are quite intelligent and capable of learning and progressing quickly. To maintain the upper hand, the trainer must always devise means of stopping the dog's shenanigans decisively. Continuing to train the dog, insisting on proper behavior as we progress, often results in a gradual lessening of contrary behavior and the emergence of a more cooperative demeanor. We recommend you do your best to control your temper and rise to the challenge of outsmarting the recalcitrant dog. Remember, you do not have to react instantly each time she invents a new stratagem. Just think up your own counter-strategy and be prepared to prevent her success the second time. We have had a number of contrary goldens, but the pattern also occurs in Labs and Chesapeakes. If your puppy shows contrary tendencies, we recommend starting obedience early. Be gentle about it, but try to get your puppy in the habit of working cooperatively at an early age.

SKIPPER

by Amy

S KIPPER WAS A "HARD LUCK" DOG. Although his breeding was excellent his litter was ill-fated. A marital break-up led to the puppies being neglected and left together. One of the few puppies to survive a parvo outbreak was given to a hunter whose main interest was bird dogs. This man offered us the puppy when it was ten months old, saying he didn't like the way it acted. If we didn't take it, he was going to have it put down.

The owner volunteered that he had kept the puppy in a kennel and did nothing with it. We knew a male Chesapeake with no history of socialization was not a good bet — but we are inclined to be softies. We agreed to take the puppy, knowing there was a significant chance we were buying heartbreak. Temperament problems arising from the lack of socialization might well necessitate our having to euthanize the puppy.

When we got the pup, he was underfed, undersized, and didn't know his name. We changed his name to Skipper, put 15 pounds on him in a matter of weeks, and discovered he was outgoing, affectionate, and eager-to-please — surprising in a puppy that had known almost total neglect. He showed a devotion typical to stray or neglected dogs that are finally given a home. He liked to retrieve and an x-ray of his hips showed that they were good, so we decided he was worth training. Skipper lived in my house in Georgia for the next six months. That was the first year of our marriage, before I quit my teaching job. I took Skipper to work with me fairly often and he got along well with the students, and of course, he rode in the truck with me on my weekend trips to visit John.

I obedience trained Skipper during the week, and worked him in the field with John's dogs on the weekends. One of the first things we tried was to throw a dead pigeon for him, since lack of bird interest is often a problem in dogs that are not introduced to birds at an early age. Skipper did not lack interest. He grabbed that pigeon and practically inhaled it. I don't remember what I did to get it away from him, but I do remember being startled at the quickness with which a dog could swallow a bird — whole. As a probable case of hardmouth, Skipper's future once again looked doubtful, but I persisted and got him force-fetched, after which his bird-handling proved to be flawless.

My next step was to teach Skipper to handle. I ran marks with him in North Carolina on the weekends, and did handling drills on the college playing fields. I had a young Lab bitch, Ariel, who was at about the same point in training. I worked the two of them on a "baseball" handling pattern, a popular method of teaching casts. Ariel picked up casting readily, but not Skipper. His forcing stood him in good stead and he understood that "over!" or "back!" coupled to a hand gesture meant "go grab a dummy." For about two months, however, Skipper simply didn't comprehend that it mattered which direction he went to get it. In retrospect, I think Skipper would have learned his casts more easily working from the force pile, as we recommend in Chapter 9.

The academic year came to an end and I moved permanently to North Carolina. Soon Skipper and Ariel were ready to begin learning "cold blinds." After a typical hacky beginning, needing twenty or thirty casts to go perhaps 200 yards, Skipper quickly emerged as a dog that loved to run blinds as he loved all retrieving. I would repeat blinds so as to follow up a choppy job with the reward of an easy run to success. If I didn't keep an eye on Skipper, he would dash back out into the field for a third dummy.

Skipper was a natural lining dog. Almost immediately he recognized that the direction in which I lined him was the direction in which he eventually found a dummy. When he understood casts as further guidance, he took his casts accurately and learned to carry them a long way. Within a very short time, Skipper would line out accurately and fast, completing 200-250 yard blinds in two or three whistles. The only trouble we had was Skipper's nose. Usually, I would set out three blinds and, if they were not far enough apart, Skipper would sometimes wind the wrong pile of dummies from 50-60 yards and need to be cast away from them.

Ariel was another story. Fast and superficially flashy, she was enthusiastic about easy retrieves but lacked Skipper's willingness to apply himself. Her lack of comprehension of being given a direction was as unusual as his genius for lining. Most dogs do not line very well at first, but she was exceptionally bad. I practiced a variety of lining drills, in an attempt to communicate that I wanted her to go in a particular direction. Still, on a cold blind, she would pick an arbitrary direction she interpreted as "back." Sometimes when I sent her, she would turn and run in the opposite direction! The problem persisted as she progressed in the field — she took her over casts well, but seemed to interpret a back cast not directly away as I intended, but as permission to head for her original destination. With much practice, I got Ariel doing decent blinds and sold her as a gun dog.

Skipper's work ethic and enthusiasm made him a pleasure to work with. Having a number of young dogs to train, though, I turned his training over to John. Skipper's new handling skills enabled him to get past a difficulty he had with tight multiple marks and to complete his honesty training. John taught Skipper to negotiate hazards such as points, angled water entries and so forth, and rapidly got him performing smoothly on Qualifying-level blinds. When we introduced retired memory birds (where the thrower hides after throwing the mark), Skipper marked them as though the guns were still visible and we started to think we had a field-trial prospect.

Skipper's introduction to retired marks came on a winter trip to Florida, during which his water work was excellent. Shortly afterwards, spring came to North Carolina and we resumed water work in the still-cold ponds and lakes around our kennel. Alas, Skipper showed a decided reluctance to retrieve in the cold water. Sometimes a program of forcing in the water can overcome this problem, and John started forcing Skipper. Although he had stood up to force-fetching and his earlier forcing on back, Skipper did not respond well to attempts to force him in the water. He went in the cold water, reluctantly, but showed a loss of confidence and of marking ability, acting worried during training.

Much as I liked the dog, it appeared that he would not have a field-trial career. Further training would entail more pressure, whether the water was cold or not, and Skipper's behavior was so characteristic of dogs who have reached their limit, we didn't hold out much hope. It was a disappointment, but having raised many young dogs we know that a dog is often outstanding in some area but has a failing which prevents it from being competitive. We decided to sell Skipper. Since being weak in cold water is a serious shortcoming in a retriever, we felt we had to accept a fairly low price. Fortunately, we received a call from an avid hunter whose main interests were early-season ducks, geese, and pheasants — not much cold-water work required. He was delighted to obtain a handling dog at a good price. He owned his own store and would take Skipper to work with him, and keep him as a house pet.

Knowing it would be hard for me to see Skipper off, John drove him to the airport. We received periodic reports from his new owner. Skipper was retrieving teal, geese, and doves. As I had anticipated, he was one of those dogs adept at figuring out what is needed in a hunting situation. A month into his first season, his owner wrote, "we have yet to lose a single bird thanks to Skipper." Skipper was effective at recovering doves lost by his owner's shooting partners, and was learning the wiles of ringneck pheasants. Later, Skipper's owner wrote, "he is one of the best retrievers I have ever seen," and described what a great family dog he was, and inseparable from their three children.

It was hard to let Skipper go, but when I reflect on his beginnings, his placement with that family is as much a success story as if he had made field champion. And every letter from his owner made me glad we decided to take on that hard-luck puppy.

CHAPTER 2

RAISING A
RETRIEVER PUPPY

Y OUR RETRIEVER'S TRAINING STARTS the day you bring him home. He is wide-eyed and ready to learn. Start now and teach him what he should know — or he will teach himself and probably get into some bad habits. If your dog already has some bad habits, recognizing the way he's learned these habits will help you apply the understanding and patience you need to overcome them.

Goals and Strategies of Socialization

Puppy training is directed toward developing behavior and abilities we desire in an adult retriever and pet. A well-trained adult retriever, in addition to having good manners, is responsive to training and to your wishes in general, confident in himself and in his master, and has initiative to solve problems of sight, scent, and terrain without depending on his master for help. His achievement in the field will depend on his *desire* — the strength of his motivation to retrieve. All of the concepts and exercises presented in this chapter are intended to develop these four qualities: *responsiveness*, *confidence*, *initiative*, and *desire*. Going overboard in pursuit of an immediate lesson is not usually compatible with these, so make a practice of using restraint. Common mistakes are emphasizing control at the expense of initiative, or the opposite — encouraging so much independence that the dog becomes hard to control. The procedures we will describe promote a good balance between the training objectives. The art of training is to maintain this balance as you adapt them to your dog.

The main strategy of puppy training is to control the environment — the stimuli and temptations that influence his behavior. While house-raising a puppy has many benefits, including the opportunity for your dog to form a strong attachment, uncontrolled elements such as family members, other dogs, frequent visitors, etc. can severely undermine your training efforts. Although this has led some authors (such as James Lamb Free) to recommend keeping your dog in a padlocked run, we consider where to keep the dog a personal choice. Since consistency is so important in teaching good behavior, if you cannot get the cooperation of everyone who comes into your house, your puppy will develop bad habits that will need to be corrected later. Raise your puppy in the house if you are so inclined — but try to enlist the cooperation of family members, and consider confining the puppy out of sight when guests are present.

Give some thought to how you want your adult dog to behave. If you have never owned a big dog before, you may be surprised at how large an adult retriever is when you share your home with one. Undoubtedly, you want him not to jump up on people. You will want him to be calm around the house. You may want him to stay off of the furniture (if this is your first big dog, we recommend this). No matter how cute it may be for a little puppy to jump up on people and race around, out of fairness to your puppy, be consistent. Do not encourage the puppy to do things

that will be forbidden when he is fully grown. The price of indul-
gence now will be a probable need for harsh reprimand later.

While directed to producing the ideal adult dog, puppy training must also be suited to a puppy! A puppy's mental, physical,
and emotional makeup is quite different than that of an adult.
His attention span is short and he quickly becomes tired and/or
distracted. Most important, he cannot possibly learn from, or
benefit by, harsh treatment. Punishment is pointless because a
young pup lacks the sophistication to understand the punishment as a consequence of his behavior. Almost everything your
puppy does is normal puppy behavior, and not done out of spite
or stubbornness. Remind yourself of this frequently! Never
strike, pinch, or intimidate your puppy, and save shouting for the
(rare) circumstance when immediate danger must be averted.

Do not expect your puppy to be rational, or to understand
what you are trying to teach him. He must be shown each step,
and will learn how to learn as you proceed with his training. For
now, the best approach is a "behavioral" one, based on positive
reinforcement. Reward desirable behavior with attention: petting, verbal praise, etc. Time these rewards to coincide with the
good behavior as closely as possible. Be on the lookout for desirable behavior: in a young puppy, sitting or standing with all four
feet on the ground while not biting is behavior you want to reinforce! When undesirable behavior occurs, interrupt it if you can
and withhold attention briefly (10 seconds). Do not think of this
as bribery; it works at an intuitive level. You can make all future
training easier by conditioning your puppy to do the things you
want him to do.

You can (and should) "engineer" your puppy's behavior.
Choosing a planned activity puts you in control and gives you
the opportunity to reward good behavior. If you take a passive
approach, letting the puppy make up his own games, you will

constantly react to his behavior by trying to correct him. Frequent and excessive use of "No!" (or other corrections) is destructive to your pup's developing confidence and initiative, and leads to the puppy's becoming less responsive.

Pay attention to situations that produce certain behavior. If you like the behavior, reward him with praise and plan to repeat the situation. If you don't, avoid the situation in order to prevent its becoming a habit. Biting at hands and clothes, for example, is more likely to occur in some situations than in others. Stopping a puppy from biting often requires a combination of several techniques; avoiding situations that seem to trigger biting is the first step. When you cannot monitor and respond to your puppy's behavior, confine him in a dog crate.

Crates

A dog crate is a necessary tool for positive-reinforcement puppy training. By confining your puppy in a crate any time he cannot be supervised, you prevent his doing most things that you would be tempted to punish and which might become bad habits. Behaviors such as destructive chewing, tearing up paper, leaping up on people, and racing around the house are *self-reinforcing*. If you are not there to supervise and put a stop to them, your puppy may condition himself to engage in them persistently. On the other hand, if the puppy is out of the crate only when you can focus your attention on him and reward proper behavior, he will quickly learn to behave acceptably. Use of a crate also makes housebreaking easier.

Introducing the crate does not have to be a big production. Your puppy will have to adapt to a life completely different than what he has known. Put him in the crate the first day, and he will accept being crated as part of his new world, not as a separate and stressful issue.

Crate-Training (Housebreaking)

Since the scheduling of your puppy's time in and out of the crate must be planned around his needs to eat and relieve himself, we will describe the basics of housebreaking by means of a crate, then turn to activities we recommend for you and your pup.

The great advantage of crate-training is that it teaches cleanliness in the house through repetition and positive reinforcement, with a minimum of failures. This avoidance of harshness is critical to bringing up a confident, resourceful puppy. It also prevents some problems that can result when punitive methods of housebreaking go awry.

Most puppies come from the breeder with a built-in aversion to lying in their own excrement. By confining your puppy in a small space, you force him to exert such control as he can muster. When you take him out, you can be (reasonably) sure he will relieve himself, allowing you the opportunity to praise him for going in the approved area. After he relieves himself, there will be a "safe" period when your puppy may be given some freedom in the house.

There are a variety of crate types available. The plastic crates used for shipping are good: they are easy to clean, and if an accident should occur in the crate, they contain it pretty well. The crate should be big enough for your puppy to lie down comfortably inside, but not much bigger. If it is big enough to define a sleeping area and a separate toilet area, your puppy may relieve himself in the crate, defeating its purpose.

Establish a place for the crate. Too much traffic or noisy activity near the crate may keep your puppy awake and emotionally wound up. A room where family members spend quiet time will provide the pup some low-key contact and prevent him from being isolated. Some authorities recommend the bedroom, which is probably ideal if it suits your lifestyle. The crate should be in a place where you can hear your puppy if he yips to get out.

Equip the crate with a washable fleece pad or something else soft for your puppy to lie on. A chew toy will give your puppy something to do while he is awake (besides making noise!).

For fastest results, air your puppy on a lead by taking him to the same spot in your yard each time. Withhold attention until he goes, then praise him and take him into the house for a short play session. At first, your puppy will have no inclination to hold his urine, so the play session needs to be very short — not over 10 minutes. After a few minutes, your puppy is no longer "safe" at large, although you can extend the social period by picking him up and holding him in your lap. When you are finished holding your puppy, put him in the crate. He will probably fuss at first, then settle down. If he later starts yammering, put the lead on and take him out to the designated spot, the same as before. After relieving himself, your puppy gets another play and attention session in the house.

Air your puppy as described first thing in the morning, after feeding, whenever you want to get him out to play or train, before bedtime, and any time he starts fussing in the crate after having been quiet. If it is the middle of the night, skip the play session. Your puppy needs to know that nighttime noise will get him one thing only: a chance to relieve himself, but no attention or playing. Water should be available any time your puppy is outside the crate — if he drinks a lot, anticipate that he will need to go out again.

You will want to gradually extend the time your puppy is at large in the house. At first, accidents are likely as a young pup will urinate with no preliminaries. When this happens, scoop your puppy up saying, "No, no, no" in a firm but not threatening tone of voice and take him outside to the usual spot. If you can, wait there until he goes again, then praise him. Clean the urine up with something that will destroy the odor. The old standby is a 1:5 solution of white vinegar in water; there are also various odor removers available from pet-supply stores. As your puppy gets older, sniffing and possibly circling will precede a "mistake." When you see these signs, whisk him outside.

A little pup will defecate almost as often as he urinates. As he gets older, this will not always be the case. Sometimes walking a pup around (and around and around) helps to get the bowels moving. If a pup defecates in the crate during the night, it may be due to loose stools or too big an evening feeding. Keep up-to-date on wormings and feed a high-quality food. If the stools are bad, take a sample to your vet for analysis.

A common mistake in housebreaking is to think that just because your puppy has been outside playing, he has recently relieved himself and is now "safe" to play indoors. More likely, he has been loafing and the change of scene will stimulate him to urinate. Either wait until you see him relieve himself again or put him in his crate.

Some puppies urinate a small-to-moderate amount when greeting their owner or a stranger, or when the owner bends over them to pet them, attach a lead, etc. This "submissive urination" is involuntary and should not be punished as a breach of house-breaking. Most pups grow out of it.

We have had dogs take anywhere from three days to six months to comprehend housetraining. Don't watch the calendar; pay attention to your dog's responses and your efforts will be effective.

Socialization and Good Manners

By establishing a routine in which your puppy is confined to a crate any time you cannot attend to him, you can ensure that his learning is under your control. This doesn't mean that you must control everything your puppy does; you control the situations in which he learns how to behave. Your discipline and organization at this stage will pay off in preventing a variety of bad habits.

When your puppy is outside of his crate, in or out of the house, bend over to pet him and give him attention. Puppies tend to want to get near your face. It's as though they're programmed to think that's the way to get attention. If you don't teach them otherwise, they will get in the habit of jumping up on people. By bending over, you reward your puppy with the attention he craves for keeping all four feet on the ground. When, in his enthusiasm, your puppy tries to jump up anyway, you can easily block the jump with a hand placed over his head to stop his upward motion. If you and all family members are

By bending down to give your puppy attention, you are simultaneously preventing jumping up and rewarding staying down.

consistent, jumping up will never become a problem. Talk to your puppy in a calm, affectionate tone of voice as you pet him. This will increase his responsiveness to you and help make verbal praise effective when you train him.

You can start teaching your puppy to sit as early as you like. A method for teaching "sit" is described in Chapter 4. Insisting that your puppy sit in order to be petted will enforce the desirable habit of keeping still, which is particularly important in high-activity puppies. Many Labrador and golden puppies are eager to take human attention as an excuse to go wild, but with a little consistency, you can counter this tendency and lay the foundation for your puppy's development of self-discipline. Around the house and in early training, you will be much happier with a puppy that has the capacity to be calm and pay attention. We keep stressing the need for consistency because it is the absolute key to success. Any behavior that is rewarded tends to recur and become persistent, so work hard to avoid rewarding your puppy with attention for jumping up or for buzzing around the house in a state of high excitement.

Introducing Retrieving

Getting your pup started retrieving is easy. Restrain him with one hand across his chest while teasing him with a good retrieving object. A knotted white sock, a canvas puppy dummy, or a rolled-up white washcloth with a rubber band or string to hold it together work well. Wiggle the object enticingly a few inches in front of your puppy's nose. When your puppy is struggling to get at the dummy, flip it forward a foot or two and release him, keeping the object in his view as you toss it. Say the word "back" as you release your puppy — this will become the command to retrieve.

Once your puppy gets the idea, you will be able to rapidly increase the distance of your throws. If you have trouble getting

Tease the puppy and get his attention on the object.

Toss the object and let your puppy go as you say, "Back."

Most puppies will pick the object up and return to you carrying it.

him to come back to you, try throwing retrieves down a hallway where the only place he can go with the dummy is back past you.

When you are ready to take the dummy, roll it gently but firmly from your puppy's mouth, or if his grip is very strong, pry up on his upper jaw with your thumb and forefinger in the gaps behind his canine teeth as you roll the dummy forward out of his mouth with your other hand.

As much fun as it is to see that short-legged, fuzzy little pup retrieving with enthusiasm, limit retrieves to only two or three per session. *This is extremely important.* Just as you will limit training sessions with your adult dog to ten minutes to maintain interest and rapid learning, keep retrieving sessions with your immature puppy correspondingly shorter. Long experience has shown that brief sessions are necessary to develop a motivated, trainable retriever.

Activities
While puppy retrieves are very important, and retrieving will become your dog's "job," it doesn't take long to throw a dummy two or three times, and your puppy needs more attention and structured time with you. We recommend several other specific activities that will further the goals of developing confidence, responsiveness, and initiative. Taking walks together is excellent. If you can find a large open area free of hazards, go for a ramble with your puppy off lead. Let him explore, sniff, investigate. As you keep moving, your puppy's attention will switch from his explorations to you, and back. If your puppy is timid, move slowly and try not to distract him from his surroundings. You want your puppy to develop confidence in his curiosity, and in his eyes and nose. If your pup is very independent, ranging far out, try running away or hiding. He will probably come after you, and pay more attention to your whereabouts in the future.

Take your puppy out to a variety of places and let him explore.

Walks on lead are also good — around the neighborhood and to places where there are people, cars, noises, etc. If you can relax and are not in a hurry, you can begin teaching your puppy not to pull. When he starts pulling, stop and don't move until the lead slackens. If you practice this, your puppy will learn that no matter how eager he is to get going, pulling won't help him. If this kind of stop-and-go progress is too frustrating for you or it doesn't seem to work with your pup, put it off until you teach him to heel. Whatever happens, do not haul your puppy along behind you. If you need to get him moving, often a short pull followed by slackening the leash and verbal encouragement will do the trick. If you are in a hurry, pick your puppy up and carry him.

You will probably use the car or truck to take your pup for walks in varied areas. This is desirable — take him for a ride as often as you can, in or out of a crate as you prefer. This is good socialization and good experience. Dogs that grow up without riding in the car may be subject to carsickness and fearfulness as adults.

The most important thing you can do to socialize a pup is to hold him. Letting him lounge in your lap is OK, but holding him against your chest with your forearm supporting his body and his legs dangling is even better. Stroke your puppy with your free hand and talk to him. Most pups struggle the first few times you do this but soon come to like it a lot.

A good way to hold a puppy. He is secure, but under your control.

Avoid Bad Habits

One activity to be avoided is free play with other dogs. Lots of people like to let their pets play with others, but it is a poor idea for a dog that is to be trained to a high level. Remember that your puppy is paying attention and learning, whatever he does. On walks with you, your puppy is learning to read your body language and also learning your importance in his life. While playing with other dogs, he will become oriented to responding to dogs, not people. Taken to excess, such play can ruin a dog for training.

We suggest you also avoid playing tug-of-war or allowing your dog to retrieve sticks. You don't want to be brought a stick after sending your dog for a difficult cripple. Tug-of-war is a competitive game. It puts you and your puppy on an equal footing. Not only does it raise the possibility, in the dog's mind, that he might keep the retrieving object, it communicates that the puppy has authority over what is in his mouth. Playing tug-of-war now may make a clean delivery harder to teach.

Chasing your dog, especially when he has a dummy or bird in his mouth, is also a bad idea, as dogs universally think "keep-away" is a great game — especially compared to the relative boredom of delivering to hand. Finally, we suggest you discourage submission displays (where the pup rolls over and lies on his back), by ceasing to pet and give your puppy attention until he stands properly upright. You will not want him to throw submission displays when you start to make demands upon him in training.

Behavior Problems

There are a few common problems that seem to be almost "built in" to retriever puppies, and which may require extra effort to control.

The most common problem people seem to have with their retriever puppies is biting. Most puppies vigorously attack and bite hands and pants' cuffs and if not discouraged, will soon progress to drawing blood. The first step to stopping this behavior is to stop encouraging it. Many inexperienced dog owners hold and move their hands near a pup's face in a manner that seems to trigger biting. Instead, pick up your puppy and hold him as described earlier. You can use your free hand on top of his head to steer him away from whatever he might try to bite. When your puppy does bite, sharply say, "Ow!" and shun him briefly (stand up or turn your back for ten seconds). Causing your puppy's fun to come to an abrupt halt is what makes this effective. Some puppies need a little more. The word "No!" accompanied by firmly holding your pup's muzzle may work; if your puppy vigorously fights your grip, you are not effectively interrupting his play. Try instead grasping him by the scruff of the neck and giving a quick, one-handed shake. Follow up by making your puppy sit if he has been taught to sit.

Destructive chewing, like puppy biting, is almost universal in retriever puppies. We suspect that this is part of the general "mouth-oriented" nature that makes retrievers love to carry things around. We have not found a satisfactory way to teach dogs not to chew. Because it is very difficult to correct any behavior after the fact, the solution is to prevent destructive chewing by avoiding leaving your puppy unsupervised in the house. The crate training procedure keeps your puppy out of trouble when he can't be supervised.

Improvement of puppy behavior varies from gradual to rapid, depending on the behavior, the puppy's personality, and the level of consistency in your household. Try to be tolerant and enjoy your puppy's youthful exuberance while gently guiding him toward good manners. Spend time on structured activities like walks and retrieving, and even if you make a few mistakes, your puppy will grow up to be people-oriented and ready for serious training.

REAL DOGS

PILOT

by John

I BOUGHT PILOT, REGISTERED AS RUM RIVER PILOT, as a seven-week-old puppy for a variety of reasons, none of them too good. I had Buck, his uncle, a year old by then and doing well in his training. Buck could do blinds and marks at great distances for that time, 1954, and I had no need to think about replacing him. It all started with a phone call from my duck hunting partner, Jerry, who said, "Say, John, I noticed in the paper an ad for Chesapeake puppies, $20 each." Well, even at that time $20 was a pretty good buy for a puppy. I had paid $40 for Buck, and for some reason, it struck me as too good a deal to pass up. So I drove to Anoka, a few miles north of my home in Minneapolis, and fell in love with the biggest, boldest pup in the litter. He rode home in my lap.

Pilot was raised in the house as a little puppy and was endearing because of his personality, which can best be described as boldly robust, and his appearance, which was huge and cuddly. His head was big and round; it seems in recollection to have been the size of a large grapefruit at seven weeks. He was built like a bulldozer, and operated like one.

We let Pilot sleep by the bed but within a week or so, his attentions in the middle of the night, pulling the covers off and other antics, led us to leave him in the kitchen for the night with the door closed. The first night we tried this, we heard a regular, loud thumping against the kitchen door — whump, whump, whump. Pilot was throwing himself against the door, but we didn't realize with what force until it stopped and Pilot came running into the bedroom, tail wagging, bubbling over with joy that he had accomplished his mission. Our apartment was in a 75-year-old building and the woodwork was of the sturdiest construction, but Pilot had managed to break the latch assembly.

Buck, at the time, was kenneled in a make-shift dog run constructed alongside the garage with a gravel floor and cheap wire stapled to wooden fence posts. I was an art student at the time with two kids and a wife to support, so extravagances for the dogs were not feasible. This kennel, if you can excuse a liberal use of the term, was what I had. It could be seen from the kitchen window of our third-floor apartment in one of the oldest neighborhoods in Minneapolis. Pilot soon got too big and rambunctious to continue as a full-time house puppy, and his destiny was to be kenneled outside with his Uncle Buck. Buck and Pilot had been introduced by this time, of course, and Pilot thought Buck was a great play-thing. He charged at Buck repeatedly, biting at his head and ears, and so forth. Buck tolerated this treatment, but was clearly none too pleased with Pilot's excess of affection. We decided one day to put them together in the kennel to see how they would get along. No sooner had we returned to our apartment than we heard an uproar — puppy screaming, Buck roaring and growling. I ran downstairs to find Pilot with his head locked in Buck's jaws. I rescued Pilot, soon enough to save his life. This was the day Pilot grew up.

Much of the training we did in those days was by trauma. Sure, it didn't make sense by today's standards, but we thought it was called for, and it worked on some dogs. Buck had been taught to handle birds properly by the trauma method. I had purchased one hen mallard in the fall and kept it loose in the garage adjacent to Buck's run. I threw the duck with feet shackled for Buck when he was about five months old. He ran across the yard to the duck and proceeded to maul and pick feathers out of it. I ran to him, wrested the duck from his mouth, gave him a shaking up, put the bird in his mouth and whacked him under the chin with my fist while shouting, "Don't you chew this duck, you S.O.B! Hold it, hold it, hold it!" That worked, and Buck was never to mishandle another bird. Why it worked, I don't know. I would never do that today. The same method was applied to Buck's attack on Pilot. "Don't you eat that puppy, you S.O.B! For God's sake, he's your nephew!" That worked, too, and the two never fought again. Pilot gave up hassling Buck, and Buck gave up trying to kill Pilot. As I said, Pilot grew up that day, and not long after achieved his full growth as a 105-pound, bear-like Chesapeake. Of course, he would have been more than a match for Buck as a full-grown dog, as Buck was a mere 80-pounder, but the pecking order had been established months before.

Pilot inherited Buck's reputation in the neighborhood as the chief heavy. Our neighbors had a large Weimaraner who liked to throw his weight around and instruct canine interlopers as to the boundary rules, which included the Weimaraner's yard and an approximate 50-yard buffer zone. My route to Cedar Lake for my daily training outings with Buck took me directly in front of the Weimaraner's house. He charged out every day to assault Buck, then a half-grown Chesapeake, and Buck, being on a leash, got quickly picked up as I shouted and kicked at the Weimaraner to "get the hell out of here." This went on until Buck was ten months old, at which point he broke away from me when the Weimaraner attacked, sailed into him and gave him a good thrashing. After that, when the Weimaraner saw Buck and me walking down the street, he would put what little tail he had between his legs and run under his porch to hide. When it came time to walk Pilot on the same route, the Weimaraner turned tail and headed for the porch. Pilot had inherited a reputation.

I soon reached the point in Buck's and Pilot's training at

which I was able to walk them to Cedar Lake (I had only a 1942 Harley Davidson motorcycle for transportation at the time) with a sack of decoys and retrieving dummies over my shoulder. I chained one dog to a tree and made the other sit and stay while I walked around a good-sized bay of the lake, 150 yards or so across, and threw out three marks. I then returned to the line and sent the sitting dog on its marks. When it was the other dog's turn, I chained the first one and trained the second in the same fashion. This was the only way I could work them both on water marks as I had no help most of the time.

The part of Cedar Lake that I trained on was a no man's land. Part of it was low and marshy with no houses, and part of it was covered with squatters' shacks which had been there since the early days of the Depression, and since the war (WWII) had been over for nearly 10 years and the economy was on the upswing, the city of Minneapolis was in the final stages of tearing down these shanties. The lake, on that end, was bordered by the Minneapolis and St. Louis switchyard, a major grain shipping terminal. One day, when I was training in this isolated and lonely setting, with Pilot chained to a good-sized bush and Buck in the midst of a marking test, a man with an Old English sheepdog suddenly appeared through the brush. This dog was not leashed and was poorly trained, if at all. The sheepdog headed for Pilot and Pilot met the challenge by uprooting the bush he was chained to and charging directly at his adversary. Buck, of course, picked up on the action, figuring that Pilot needed his support, which he didn't, but comrades in arms stick together. They would have made quick work of the sheepdog, but we were able to get them separated. The man with the sheepdog was very nice, and retreated quietly, but that was the last time I saw him on "my training grounds." Chesapeakes have a legendary reputation as proficient fighters. It is well earned.

Pilot became a powerful 105-pounds of bone and muscle by the time he was about a year old. His athletic abilities were astounding. By then I had given Buck to a close friend because of a foot injury he suffered while training. Pilot was my only dog, and the sole occupant of his dog run. Pilot didn't like it when Buck left and was lonely. He took to jumping the fence of his kennel whenever the mood struck him. He would stay in for a day or two, then I'd look out the window and see him sitting in that leap-crouch of his, visually measuring the kennel wire height, which was over six feet. After a few moments of observation, up he would go in a smooth, panther-like leap over the top and out. I thought that by adding extensions on the fence posts, and increasing the height to eight and a half feet, I could keep him in, but the same thing was repeated — he'd look up, crouch for a few seconds, and. . . over the top. I finally solved the problem by roofing the kennel with wire. After bumping his head against that a few times, he gave up trying to jump out.

Pilot's ability to leap could be applied to various cute activities, such as leaping straight up, as high as I could hold a dummy, to grab it from my hand. I also contrived a small practical joke, funny only to me, in which Pilot, on the command "Pilot," would jump into the window of a parked vehicle, gracefully avoiding a collision with the door window frame. I enjoyed doing this when someone pulled up in front of my house to converse from the driver's seat of their car or pickup. I would tell Pilot to sit and he would remain perfectly still during the conversation. When I said "Pilot," he would spring through the window into the lap of the driver. I laughed, but my friends usually said something like, "That's the stupidest dog trick I've ever seen!"

Buck stayed with a friend in Minneapolis and Pilot went with me to my first teaching job in Jamestown, ND, in 1959. North

Dakota had a bountiful duck population at the time, but my first year there was marked by some memorable extremes in weather. The day we moved I struggled in 100° heat and a 70-mile-an-hour dust storm to put up a dog run — a matter of primary importance. This was in early September. The opening day of duck hunting, in early October, saw temperatures in the seventies, and balmy conditions prevailed. On the second or third day of the duck season, the temperatures plummeted into the teens and we had a heavy snow, so it looked like our duck hunting was over for the year. All the shallow sloughs and potholes froze over, not to open up until the following spring. My only hope for duck hunting was the one deep-water lake in the area, Spiritwood Lake, 12 miles north of my home.

Spiritwood Lake stayed open most of the season and we enjoyed many good shoots, mostly on bluebills from a rocky point. As we approached the end of the season in mid-November, Spiritwood, too, froze over except for a tiny hole in the ice about 10' in diameter, 200 yards from shore. The morning we hunted under these conditions, we noticed that the patch of open water in the middle of the lake was full of ducks, all of them bluebills. Pilot, surprisingly at that distance, saw the ducks too, and when we weren't expecting it, took off over the ice toward the ducks. When he got to the hole in the ice, all of the ducks disappeared suddenly. They dove. Pilot stood on the edge of the hole looking perplexed. Soon, ducks began to pop up to the surface for want of air. When one would come up close enough to the edge of the ice, Pilot would grab it and bring it to us. The fourteenth duck dove, and Pilot went into the water after it. He caught the duck by diving himself — Pilot was a very good diver, and would disappear beneath the water's surface for several seconds. He surfaced with the bluebill in his mouth and found he couldn't get up on the ice.

Clearly, the only thing to do was to save the dog, no matter what the risk. Fortunately, near us was a small boat that had been turned over for the winter. Curt, my hunting partner, and I turned it right-side-up and started to push it out on the ice toward the stranded dog. We figured if we began to break through with our sled-like boat, we could jump in and continue to break the ice with an oar. We hoped we could make it to Pilot before he gave out. Almost immediately after we launched the boat we saw Pilot, the duck still in his mouth, slide that big head and chest out onto the ice as far as he could extend it. This was followed by a hind leg coming out and hooking its toenails on the edge of the ice. Pilot then clambered out onto the ice and brought the fourteenth bluebill home. I had saved Buck in a similar situation by breaking a return path through the ice with a fence post in chest-deep water. Pilot, however, relieved us of trying to meet that responsibility, with potentially fatal consequences..

When we got home and dressed the 14 bluebills, none of which we had shot, we found they were all cripples in various states of disrepair. Most had broken wings; some had festering body wounds. We cleaned them up as best we could and had bluebills for supper every night for a week.

In remembering Pilot and his feats of physical endurance and strength, I don't think I have seen another dog who could pull himself out of swimming-depth water onto the ice. Pilot later went to Florida as the chief retriever of a 1,700-acre duck hunting preserve, never to face such conditions again.

CHAPTER 3

FIELD WORK
WITH YOUR PUPPY

T HE PRIMARY GOAL OF ALL PUPPY work should be to condition your puppy to love retrieving. While many training procedures for adult retrievers use force, it is the positive reinforcement of making the retrieve that keeps the dogs working, and working happily, under force and pressure. We call it *desire*. Any experienced trainer will tell you that a dog who lacks desire has limited potential. The more retrieving desire a dog has, the faster she learns, the farther she can ultimately progress, and the more fun she is to train, to hunt, and to watch.

You can and should start your puppy retrieving as soon as possible, using play retrieves to build your puppy's desire (her love of retrieving) to the most intense level possible.

Every retrieving session needs to be planned around the primary goal of building desire, and any immediate purpose that conflicts with this goal must be avoided. For example, almost all puppies decide, at some point, not to bring back the dummy or bird. You could train your pup rigorously to come when called, then call her in on a retrieve — but even if she doesn't drop the dummy on the way in, her enthusiasm will be dampened. Remember, a puppy's mind is very simple. While you are full of plans for her future, she only knows that retrieving is a fun game. If you start imposing rules, you may take the fun away. Later, we will detail some strategies for getting the puppy back without discouraging her.

The first key to building up the positive-reinforcing power of the retrieve is to prevent your puppy from getting bored. Remember — two or three throws per session. Yes, most puppies would happily retrieve all day — but all of them will lose interest with repeated long sessions. If your puppy's attention starts to wander, or after a retrieve she drops the dummy and goes exploring, you've done too much. Plan to do fewer throws next time.

Try to maintain a high success rate, 100 percent if possible. Your puppy needs to develop confidence that if she sees something fall, she can make the retrieve. As your puppy learns "the business," you will want to gradually increase distance, throw marks in cover, and generally provide more of a challenge. If she has trouble with a retrieve, or if she finds the dummy or bird after a long hunt, resist letting your pride make you repeat the challenge. Throw a mark you know she will find easily. Make sure your puppy is always rewarded, not discouraged.

As you progress in distance and difficulty, make sure your puppy's retrieves are not too demanding physically. Swimming is harder work than running, so retrieves in water should be shorter than on land. If your puppy charges through some brush or briars, great — but don't repeat that throw; give her another throw in a less difficult location. Do not have your puppy retrieve from cold water. You will build more toughness later on by not expecting toughness now.

Throughout puppyhood, continue to restrain your pup when you (or a helper) throw marks, releasing her with a "back" command *when the dummy is almost to the ground.* This restraint builds focus and desire far better than throwing with the puppy unrestrained. Steadiness (the dog is responsible for sitting still until sent)

Restrain your puppy while a mark is thrown with a hand on the collar and, if necessary, a hand on her back making her sit.

is better left until after force-fetching. For now, keep your puppy's job simple by letting her concentrate on getting to her dummy or bird without having to worry about other responsibilities.

Some people prefer to send their dog on her name. Many field trialers use their dog's name to send on marks, and "back" for blinds as a cue to help their dogs distinguish between them. We find, however, that using the dog's name as a command to retrieve creates some confusion in early training. As we use a dog's name in a variety of situations, we prefer to keep training simple and have a command specifically for sending the dog. This is useful when introducing a new situation, such as double marks. Whatever command you choose, use it on every retrieve as you let your puppy go.

Although a good retriever always seems as though nothing could deter her from getting the bird, in reality, the trainer should never

With a young puppy who is already retrieving, it usually takes only one or a few tries before she will pick up the bird and carry it enthusiastically.

take retrieving desire for granted. Training sessions must always be planned so the immediate goal can be reached without discouraging your dog. The training procedures we will present can all be applied in this way. For now, your retriever's puppyhood is your golden opportunity to build her desire, and her ultimate potential.

Introducing Birds

A good retriever has not only an abundance of drive, but also a powerful bird desire, or *birdiness*. No matter how much a dog likes retrieving, she will not hunt hard for a lost or crippled bird unless she is birdy. We find that introducing retrievers to birds while they are still puppies results in the development of enthusiasm for birds. Neglecting to do so can lead to a lack of bird interest.

We like to start out with a freshly-killed pigeon. Tease your puppy with the pigeon briefly, then toss the pigeon about the same distance you throw the dummy, keeping the bird in your puppy's view as you throw. If you hold the pigeon by the wings, extended and held together over its back, and put a little spin on it as you throw, it will flap enticingly. Release your puppy. If she doesn't pick up the bird, perhaps sniffing it a little, go pick it up and promptly toss it again (from where it fell the first time). Resist the temptation to vocally encourage your pup — before she picks up the bird, your voice is likely to distract her. Throw the bird up to a half-dozen times if she continues not to pick it up, then put it away and try again tomorrow. Don't throw the dummy again for your pup until she has retrieved the bird. Few puppies need more than two or three days of this to start retrieving birds, and quickly become bird-crazy.

Most likely, your puppy will start grabbing the bird eagerly by the third toss, if not sooner. She is apt to decide quickly that she likes the bird even better than her dummy, so that getting her back and getting the bird away from her may be a challenge. Do not worry too much if she grips the bird so tightly as to cause damage. This is common and usually disappears after the adult teeth come in. If your puppy is reluctant to release the bird, often

You can usually get a bird away from a puppy if you pick her up.

picking her up will cause her to drop the bird or at least relax her grip enough for you to get the bird. If you must pry your puppy's mouth open, be careful not to pinch her lips against her teeth or otherwise cause pain.

Once your puppy is going eagerly for the bird and snatching it up without any preliminary sniffing, go back to using dummies and throw birds only about once every week or two. Exposure to birds at this frequency will cause most puppies' enthusiasm to grow by leaps and bounds. More frequent use of birds can lead to unruliness, as the puppy plays with the bird, runs off, or lies down to chew on it. If you have these problems, use birds less frequently.

Introducing a Thrower

As soon as your puppy can retrieve as far as you can throw, it is time to teach her to retrieve from a thrower. This will enable you to extend her range, and also teach her to direct her attention out into the field where the action is. If you can get a reliable helper, we feel it is preferable to have a human thrower, rather than a mechanical launcher, at this stage. It is extremely important that your young puppy succeed on all of her retrieves, and a live thrower can help your puppy when she is confused and in danger of failing. If good help turns out to be hard to find and you need to use a mechanical launcher, always try to plan in advance how you will help your puppy if she has trouble with a mark.

There are various ways to set up a puppy's first throws. One is to have the thrower stand the distance of a short throw in front of you and off to one side while you restrain your puppy. On your signal, the thrower calls, "Hey, hey!" and throws the dummy across in front of you. This way, the fall is closer to you than to the thrower, which may help your puppy get the idea of returning to you, not your helper. It helps if the thrower watches your puppy to make sure she is looking at him or her. Instruct your thrower not to swing the dummy as a preliminary to throwing. A simple throw is sufficient. When the dummy is almost on the ground, release your puppy. When she finds the dummy, start whistling and calling her back.

Usually it only takes one session for a puppy to learn the pattern of watching the thrower, retrieving, and returning to you. Then you can start increasing your puppy's range by having the thrower stand farther away. Remember, though, that being smaller than an adult, your puppy will not be able to go very far without tiring. You need to watch for signs of confusion or waning enthusiasm, especially in hot weather. Do not get discouraged if this occurs — your puppy's muscles and lungs are still growing — just work at distances where she maintains enthusiasm. Vary the distance within your puppy's comfortable range so she doesn't develop the habit of stopping at the same distance all of the time.

Instruct your thrower clearly. Throws should be underhand, with a high arc to make them visible, and should be thrown at right angles to the line between you and the thrower, i.e. to right or left but not towards or away from you. If you repeat a throw (which we recommend only if your puppy has difficulty in finding the dummy), throw the second dummy in the same spot as the first. Otherwise, make sure throws are well separated, or your puppy may become confused.

In your efforts to challenge your puppy, you are likely to throw a mark she cannot find on her own. Before she gets lost, have your thrower help her. Most often, at this level, a puppy will

Suggested configuration for introducing throws from a helper.

H = *handler*
D = *dog*
T = *thrower*
X = *spot where dummy lands*

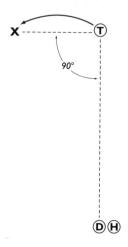

stray from the area of the fall after failing to find her object. If your puppy is abandoning the area of the fall, cue the thrower to assist. The thrower should be previously instructed to say, "Hey, hey!" and throw a second dummy to the same spot where the first one fell, the instant your puppy turns to look. If your puppy doesn't look immediately, the thrower should keep calling until she does, then throw. Timing is important, so your helper should have a dummy ready in hand and be watching for your cue.

If you can get one person to throw for your pup consistently, you can work out a set of signals for different kinds of help. Sometimes, on marks in the water, a puppy loses sight of a dummy due to her low eye level and the angle of the light. Navigation in water is an acquired skill for most dogs, and marking an unseen dummy may be too great a challenge for a puppy. All the youngster needs in this situation is a repeat throw to make a splash right by the first one — a shout calling her attention to the throwing location probably will confuse her. In other circumstances (usually with a more sophisticated dog), a simple "Hey, hey" from the thrower is sufficient for the puppy to get oriented and remember the location of the fall. If your thrower is ready and watching for your cue, you can have him or her shout, shout and throw, or throw, with the timing necessary to save your puppy from failure.

It is important that your thrower be visible. Your puppy cannot mark what she cannot see, and she won't see the fall if she doesn't know where to look. White contrasts with most backgrounds. Include an oversized white shirt in your training kit and you can make sure your thrower is visible no matter what he or she wears on a particular day. Some people criticize this practice because there are no white-shirted throwers on a typical duck hunt. But this criticism misses the point of training. Training involves building up the skills and the confidence needed to be a competent retriever. Building confidence requires success, and coaching requires knowing the challenges a dog faces — and we must know that she sees the marks. Learning to watch for birds in "real hunting situations" is an easy adjustment, as is adapting to the hidden throwers often used in hunting tests.

White dummies are ideal for puppy work in most situations, and are visible on the ground in short cover — great for building confidence. Eventually you will want your puppy to use her nose to hunt up a dummy or bird, but in early puppyhood it works well to have the visual cue of the thrown dummy followed up by a highly-visible dummy on the ground.

Introducing the Gun

As soon as your puppy is familiar with marking falls from a thrower and is retrieving out to fifty yards or so, we recommend you begin using a blank pistol. Pistols firing 22-caliber blanks or shotgun primers are loud enough to hear at any range likely in training. Your helper will need hearing protection. At first, have the thrower fire the pistol, shout "Hey-hey!" and throw a dummy. The report of a firearm is a brief impulse of sound that is hard to locate, and your puppy is apt to look around in confusion on hearing the shot. The "Hey-hey!" is needed to help return her attention to your thrower. After practicing this for a few days, your puppy will start to look in the direction of the shot, and you can omit the "Hey-hey!". It is useful, though, if the thrower watches your pup and is prepared to shout before throwing any time she looks in the wrong direction.

Although dogs can develop an ability to look in the direction of a shot, it is never foolproof. Dogs are readily confused in situations where the firing pin falls on a dud or an empty chamber, and the gun is re-cocked and fired after the mark is on the ground. Typically they look around wildly, and even after seeing the fall, may prove unable to come up with the mark, especially if the report causes an echo. This problem can be prevented by always firing the pistol prior to throwing. If it fails to fire, the thrower can re-cock it and try again, or shout before throwing (in the case of forgetting to reload). The throw should commence immediately after the shot, as the dog's confidence in the direction of the shot may falter, causing her to look away if no throw is evident.

This pattern of work — having marks from a thrower preceded by a shot — teaches the dog to look in the direction of a gunshot quickly enough to see a falling bird. While a blank pistol is not a shotgun, a few sessions using a shotgun will suffice to get your dog to look as eagerly in the direction of a shotgun blast as she looks for a blank shot — especially if a shotgun means a bird. Use of a thrower orients your puppy to expecting action to originate "out there," not from you, and is good preparation for many common dove, pheasant, and duck-hunting situations. It is, of course, also the pattern used in all field trials and most hunting tests. In addition, use of a thrower gives the trainer complete control over the training setup.

Introduction to Water
A duck dog, field-trial or hunt-test dog will do much of her work in the water. Her attitude toward water can have a profound effect on her achievement. Throughout training, therefore, we make sure the dog's experiences in the water involve a minimum of unpleasantness. Water work is inherently challenging without added ordeals to endure. Physical discomfort arises mainly from

cold water and corrections made while your dog is in the water, although submerged hazards, especially upon water entry, can be discouraging as well as dangerous. Common sense dictates that dogs should be worked in cold water very little, for short distances, and only when they are advanced in their training. Water training sessions should be planned, anticipating refusals or confusion in such a way that physical correction in the water can be kept to a minimum. And, of course, your pup's first exposure to water should be pleasant.

There are different methods for introducing a puppy to water. You don't want to risk her refusing to retrieve, so don't start by throwing a dummy out into swimming-depth water. Instead, after you have had your puppy a week or more and she is attached to you, try wading out into a pond with a gently sloping bottom. Call, cheer, clap, and do whatever you can to encourage her to follow you voluntarily. Most puppies will follow fairly readily, and if you wade into slightly deeper water, will start swimming with confidence. Very small puppies have a hard time getting a grip on a floating dummy, but if your dog is three months or older, you can try tossing a dummy a few feet in front of her as she swims (throw toward deeper water as your puppy will probably head for shore once she gets the dummy in her mouth).

Once your puppy can do a retrieve of this kind, she is ready for throws from the water's edge. These should initially be short so the puppy is only swimming for a few feet. You can gradually lengthen the distance. One good way to introduce these initial short swims is to stand back from the edge so your puppy can run a little way before getting in the water. Keep in mind that your puppy will not be able to see the dummy from very far away. Be careful to increase distances gradually.

If your puppy is unwilling to follow you into the water, or the water temperature is below 60° or so, you will need to wait until

Wade in and try to entice your puppy to follow.

Most young puppies will swim after you with little hesitation.

Once your puppy is swimming, try a short retrieve right where you stand.

Once your puppy is retrieving from the shore, you can gradually increase the distance.

she is older. We keep trying every couple of weeks, but some puppies just won't go swimming on their own. A treatment we have used successfully on puppies of four months and older is to wade out to swimming-depth water carrying the puppy, set her down, and let her swim. Generally puppies will swim back to shore, but some, when they realize they can swim, will come back out to you if you call. If your puppy doesn't come back, go get her and wade out once more, bringing a dummy. Set the puppy down in the water holding her collar, tease her with the dummy, and toss the dummy four or five feet ahead (away from shore). Two or three retrieves of this kind and your puppy will probably be ready for short retrieves in the water.

Another way to get a pup started on retrieves from water is to throw dummies for her to retrieve in shallow water where she can run all the way out and back. After a session or two of this kind, many puppies will readily swim those last few feet to get a dummy.

Depending on the size of pond, you may soon progress to the point where your puppy can swim all the way across after a thrown dummy. By this time, your puppy is probably retrieving marks thrown in cover on land, and it is tempting to see if she

Sooner or later, most puppies fall for the temptation of an easy and obvious land route.

Having run all the way, a puppy may be slow or reluctant to enter the water at the end.

can mark a dummy that lands out of sight on the opposite shore. It is best to put this off, and have your thrower continue to throw dummies that land in the water. For the sake of visibility, these should be angled right or left, not thrown directly toward you. Once a puppy gets out of the water on the far shore and has her dummy, it can be very difficult to get her back across the pond. Hitting the water in order to make a retrieve, and hitting the water a second time to return to you, are quite different. Avoiding the swim by running around the water could be the beginning of a very undesirable habit — cheating.

Set up a good puppy water mark with no obvious temptation . . .

. . . and the same puppy goes straight and hits the water hard — habits you want to develop.

Preventing Cheating

A working retriever marks much better if she goes straight to her bird instead of taking a devious route. It is also infinitely more appealing to watch a dog who appears focused on getting her bird than one intent on finding an easy way, i.e. cheating. In extreme cases, the shirker, or cheater, is so entrenched in her avoidance of water that she takes off down the shore at right angles to the direction of the fall, and refuses the retrieve if she cannot find a land route. Sooner or later, every motivated retriever puppy will realize that she can get to certain marks faster by running around, so the trainer must teach her to be "honest," and go straight.

As with housebreaking and manners, the best approach with a young puppy is to provide opportunities to practice the desired habit and prevent opportunities to indulge in the undesirable ones. When your puppy is older, you can address the problem of honesty more directly. For now, set up water marks that do not include much temptation to cheat by making sure there is no obvious land route to the destination. Marks thrown across long, narrow ponds or channels are ideal. Continue to make sure the water is warm and the distances are not so great as to discourage your puppy.

Retrievers can cheat cover and other obstacles as well as water. The effect is similar, causing inaccuracy and failure on marks and encouraging the dog to act wimpy instead of courageously driving for the mark. When working across a change of cover, or an obstacle such as a road or ditch, work from close to the obstacle and straight across (so the line to the mark is at right angles to the edge of the new cover or the line of the road). When the puppy is proficient at crossing the obstacle or line of cover, you can try throwing marks across it at an angle, close to you, and running straight across, from farther back. The more extreme the angle of approach and the farther away the obstacle, the more likely your puppy will turn and run along it rather than crossing.

Some dogs seem predisposed to be "water-freaks." They may or may not be willing to go in the water on their own as puppies, but once they learn that they can swim, it becomes very hard to get them out of the water. They are apt to swim back and forth, splashing the water with their forepaws, yipping and snapping at the splashing water. Even dogs who come when called in other circumstances usually ignore calls and whistles once they start water-freaking, and the trainer has the choice of going in after

Adult Cheasapeake water-freaking. This dog will not retrieve in the water.

The long cord is needed to get her out of the water.

the dog or waiting until she gets bored and comes out on her own — which may be 45 minutes or more.

Water-freaking is common in Chesapeakes but rare in Labradors. It is not usually a training problem in Labs, but in Chesapeakes it can get out of hand if not managed. The worry is that the desire to play in the water will come to rival the desire to retrieve, making reliable water retrieving impossible, particularly when the dog does not have the motivation of seeing the fall (blind retrieves). As with other potential behavior problems, the most important tactic is to prevent opportunities to develop the habit. You may be able to do short water retrieves where the dummy is obvious to your puppy, or you may need to keep her away from water altogether until after she comes reliably when called and has been force-fetched. At that time, you will be able to command your dog to retrieve and to come back, and if she fails to do either, her training will give you the means to compel her to behave properly.

The Art of Getting Your Puppy to Come Back

"How can I get my puppy to come back to me on retrieves?" is probably the most often-asked question in retriever work. While usually the inquirer is looking for a short simple answer, getting puppies to come back is an ongoing challenge that lasts up to the age of six months and beyond. Most good retriever puppies want to keep the retrieving object, especially if it is a bird, and sooner or later get the idea of not bringing it back to you. A puppy may

Running off with a bird is a common problem.

head the other way with the dummy in her mouth, dance around out of reach, or lie down with a possessive paw over the dummy (and possibly chew on it). Don't get angry; this is a good sign, and perfectly normal. It will, however, require patience and ingenuity to work through the not-coming-back stage.

The catch-22 of puppy retrieving is that using force to train your puppy to return is apt to discourage her from retrieving, but if you can't get the puppy to come back, you can't work on developing her retrieving desire. Fortunately, we have an array of techniques to keep getting puppies back to us until they are old enough for enforcement of the "here" command. The key to most of them is engineering, as with developing good habits in the house.

Puppies have a built-in chase response. If you chase your puppy, she will run away. The positive reinforcement of play-chasing (especially playing keep-away with the dummy) is very strong. We have seen puppies who ceaselessly harass other dogs,

If you run away, your puppy will probably chase you — bringing the dummy with her.

*Throw in a direction
that will place you
between your puppy
and the place she wants
to go, such as a gate or
vehicle.*

the cat, etc. to try to get one to chase them, leaping away with
great glee when somebody finally does. On the other hand, if you
run away, your puppy is apt to chase you, whether she has a
dummy in her mouth or not. Wherever you are, if your puppy
looks like she might not come back, turn and head the other way.
Hiding behind a tree or other object also often works.

Sometimes kneeling down, arms wide apart, is enough to
attract a puppy. Praising your puppy in an excited tone of voice,
clapping your hands, and blowing multiple short blasts on a
whistle, all attract most pups. We do all of these, continuously,
from the time a young pup picks up the dummy or bird until we
can get our hands on her. It helps to establish that when you call
your puppy in an excited tone of voice, she can get praise, attention, and/or treats by coming to you. In addition, petting and
praising the puppy while she stands with the dummy in her
mouth may keep her from thinking that returning to you means
having her prize snatched away.

Most puppies come straight back to shore on water retrieves.

You can't throw a retrieve just anywhere and expect your puppy to come back. Instead, throw retrieves in places from which she is likely to want to return. Young puppies, up to about three months and sometimes more, usually have a particular place they want to go to, and if you get between them and it, you can catch them (especially if they are dragging a check cord). They tend to head for familiar territory. Out in the field, typically, they want to go under the car or truck, so always throw out away from the vehicle. At home, if you have part of your yard fenced near the house, stand near the open gate and throw out away from it. Almost all puppies in this situation will head back for the gate, although as your puppy gets older and smarter you may need to stand far enough to one side for her to think she can dart past you.

If you don't have a gate, you can try the "head 'em off at the pass" technique. While any move toward the pup may trigger a game of keep-away, running on an intercept course doesn't seem to — and often you can get away with this ruse for weeks before your puppy figures it out.

As your puppy gets older, faster, and smarter, and you are working on longer retrieves, sooner or later you will need a new tactic. If it is warm enough for water work, practice retrieves straight out into the water. Almost all retriever puppies swim straight back to shore before trying to head in another direction. If you meet your puppy at the water's edge before she has a chance to duck away, you may get your feet wet but you will also be able to get the dummy from her mouth before she can shake, preventing the bad habit of dropping dummies.

Retrieving from cover has almost the same effect as retrieving from water. Puppies tend to head straight back out of the cover towards you. The throw may need to be shortened so the pup can find the dummy or bird easily, and needs to be straight into the area of cover, not angled. If you live in an area where foxtails

If nothing else works, you can use a long check cord.

or other grass awns are a problem, be aware that getting one of these up her nose can be fatal, so do not send your puppy into an area where she will have to hunt among them. Longer retrieves can also have the effect of making your puppy more inclined to return, possibly because she is farther out in unfamiliar territory.

For land retrieves in medium-short cover you may need to use a long check cord. We have a 100-foot check cord we use with committed "runners." We keep throws within this distance, and take up the slack as the puppy returns. Usually this requires backing up to keep the puppy's feet from fouling the cord — a very awkward procedure at first but one most people can learn with practice.

While you can certainly introduce the "here" command with a young puppy and practice it in a controlled situation, we recommend that you wait until after she is six months old to insist on total reliability. Never command "here" on a retrieve before your puppy is reliable because if she does not come, you are in a no-win situation: you must either allow her to disregard the "here" command, or you must enforce the command in a way that will punish her for retrieving. Either way you may undo a lot of careful work.

We use all of these tactics regularly. Sometimes, though, we train a puppy for which none of them work. We may get to our last-resort strategy of the long check cord and find that the puppy spits out the dummy in response to the coercion of the cord. If this happens repeatedly, take a break from retrieving for a week, continuing your puppy's other activities, then try again. Puppies progress through a lot of "phases," and a week can bring a noticeable change in attitude and behavior. If it doesn't, try waiting another week.

Lab puppy showing an eager hunt for an unseen dummy.

Encouraging Development of a Hunt

While the skill of marking justly receives a lot of attention, hunting aggressively, persistently, and effectively for a fallen dummy or bird is also a necessary skill in a retriever. We usually notice puppies starting to show a little hunt around the age of thirteen weeks or after. At first, they may walk a couple of steps looking for the dummy using their eyes. If this leads to success, the tendency to hunt will be rewarded. As you work with a thrower to extend your puppy's range, and start throwing marks in light cover, be ready to have your thrower help your puppy before she gives up hunting. Adjust the difficulty level so that she rarely needs such help.

Most puppies learn to hunt using their noses without any special attention to the issue on the part of the trainer. Once in a while, though, a puppy will come along who habitually relies on her eyes alone, up to the age of four or five months and beyond. With these dogs, we recommend a drill suggested by D. L. Walters. Hide a pan of dog food (moistened kibble) in a field with some cover. Go for a stroll in the field with your puppy.

Saunter along a few yards downwind of the food. When your puppy shows signs of catching the scent, be quiet and unobtrusive so as not to distract her from using her nose to investigate. In the case of a puppy who has never learned to use her nose, it can be pretty amusing to watch as she catches and loses the scent. When she finds the food, allow her to eat. Repeat this procedure the next day with the food hidden elsewhere in the field, and don't walk so close to it (give your puppy a little more initiative). It usually doesn't take very many days of this drill for puppies to become adept at using their noses. If your puppy will pick up and retrieve a dummy or bird she finds on the ground, switch to using one of these in place of the dog food. Continue to hide it in different places, and your pup will soon become oriented to hunting with her nose.

Some trainers advocate training a dog forcibly to stay in the "area of the fall," using the electric collar to punish her for leaving the area. We feel it is preferable to do all we can to develop a dog's inclination to hunt positively for the bird, rather than emphasizing the negative "don't leave."

Teething

Puppies begin teething somewhere around the age of four months, and react in a variety of ways. Some seem unaffected — doing everything as before, and remaining gung-ho about retrieving — but may bring the dummy back covered with blood. Others don't show discomfort, but suddenly seem uninterested in picking up the dummy. On the first retrieve, a pup may pick up the dummy, but on the way back repeatedly drop it, hold it sloppily, or abandon it a few feet in front of you. On the second retrieve, she may run to the dummy but not pick it up. If you throw a third retrieve, she may not go at all. Obviously, you are not doing this puppy any good by throwing dummies for her!

You can try fresh dead birds as long as your pup handles them well, or a soft canvas dummy, or just take a break from retrieving for a few weeks.

Some pups show the more extreme reaction of acting "down" and overly sensitive while teething. If your puppy reacts this way, back off on the obedience. Concentrate on taking your puppy for walks and exposing her to new sights and smells until the sensitivity passes.

Introducing Multiple Marks

We like to try to teach puppies to do hand-thrown doubles (and sometimes triples), in which the trainer throws his own dummies. Some dogs have difficulty learning to do a double after force-fetching and extensive practice on singles. The concept of retrieving something the dog did not just see fall is basic to blind-retrieve work as well as to "memory birds," so we like to introduce it early.

Hold your puppy by the collar while you toss a dummy out a short distance, making sure it is visible in short cover. Then turn almost 180 degrees and toss a second dummy in the other direction, sending your puppy when the second dummy is almost on the ground. If your puppy heels on your left, the mechanics are a little easier if you throw the right-hand throw first. As your puppy returns she will be facing the first dummy and should see it. Catch your puppy and get the dummy from her, then point her in the direction of the remaining dummy (the first one thrown). When your puppy makes a move indicating her attention is on the dummy, immediately let her go and give your command to retrieve ("back" or your puppy's name). Tuck the first dummy out of sight, in a pocket or under your arm, as soon as you take it from your puppy. In multiple marks and in later drill work, dummies lying on the ground can cause confusion and interfere with getting your puppy's attention focused where you want it.

Puppies develop the sophistication to do a multiple retrieve at different ages. It seems to "switch on" quite suddenly, usually after four months of age, so if your puppy doesn't get the idea the first time you try it, wait a couple of weeks and try again. On the other hand, if your puppy seems eager to grab and deliver a dummy she spots lying on the ground, she is probably ready to try a little double.

Once your puppy gets "in the groove" of looking immediately at the remaining dummy when she returns with the first one, you can try making the throws a little longer, so the memory dummy is out of sight. Don't get so carried away by practicing doubles that you neglect your puppy's work on singles, however. Most marking concepts can best be learned as singles, and developing your puppy's range and resourcefulness is at least as important as getting her memory going.

You will probably be tempted to try a triple if your puppy grasps doubles well. Your triple will become an exercise in chaos, however, unless your puppy returns well and delivers well. Usually dogs find it easiest to pick up the center throw last, so make that one a little longer and, as your puppy returns with her first retrieve, face the dummy on the opposite side to help focus her attention there. As she returns with the second dummy, face the center one, and wait for a sign of recognition before sending her. If she picks up the triple successfully, great — but don't repeat because you have used up your puppy's quota of three retrieves. Go practice singles for a few days!

Continue using play-retrieves to build your dog's enthusiasm until she is six to eight months old and has completed formal obedience, and you are ready to force fetch.

REAL DOGS

TAR OF MOON LAKE

by John

TAR WAS A PUPPY WHO, although he showed a lot of retrieving instinct, didn't want to get in the water. He was unfortunate to be born during the frigid season in North Dakota, which is most of the year, and was not introduced to water until he was about eight months old. I took Tar to the water's edge of a little slough one afternoon when things had warmed up in late spring. Tar had no more than gotten his feet wet when he lifted them up as if he had stepped on something hot, and backed away from the water with an expression of extreme distaste. I knew then that he wasn't a natural water dog.

Tar had the breeding to be a good water dog. His mother, Nodak Bonnie Girl, was a dynamo in the water, no matter how cold, and was a granddaughter of the great National Field Champion Marvadel Black Gum. His father, Ace High Flush, was a fine water dog of good field-trial breeding who belonged to a close friend. So how come Tar was a wimp in the water? I don't know, but he was what I had, so I embarked on a training program to make a water dog of him.

My efforts to make water fun for Tar fell flat. I carried him into the water, threw pigeons in the water, waded out and tried to cajole him into swimming, but none of these efforts paid off. Why I went to such lengths to see Tar through his negativism about the water I don't remember — possibly it was because he was such a brilliant and attractive youngster in all other respects. Also, I was a young college professor and, of course, knew everything. I could not accept the proposition that Tar might be inherently unable to do everything a retriever was supposed to do.

My next efforts to get Tar to swim were delayed until I had him sufficiently force fetched so that I could send him for any object and he would run out, pick it up, and return with a perfect delivery sitting at my left side. He became so good at this that I could hide a dummy anywhere in our yard, which consisted of several acres, get Tar out and say "back" to him, and he'd cover the entire property in less than a minute and be back on the dead run with a dummy. Later, we perfected the flying delivery, which he would do whenever I held my hand over my head as he was returning. This consisted of my holding a hand aloft when Tar reached a point about 20 feet in front of me on his return. He would leave the ground about 10 feet out, placing the bird or dummy in my hand on the fly. It was quite a spectacle, and I used to do it once in a while at field trials, mostly just club stuff, to show off.

This is as far as I pursued Tar's forcing back on land. My next job was in the water. I took Tar to a small pond, no more than 30 feet across, and threw a dummy into the middle. I sent Tar on the back command and, as would be expected, he ran down to the water's edge, stopped, and pondered how he could get the dummy and stay dry at the same time. It was at this time that I introduced him to the training stick, a length of broomstick about 2 feet long. This tool, by the way, and a whistle, were the only pieces of equipment used to train Tar. The e-collar was in its infancy, and trainers were doubtful of its value. Tony Berger, the great trainer of National Field Champions Cork of Oakwood Lane and Del-Tone Colvin, once said of the e-collar, "If you can't train a dog without it, you can't train one with it." That was considered axiomatic at the time.

The whacks on the rump with the training stick worked and the frequency with which it had to be applied diminished rapidly. It got to the point where I could send Tar through high cover, woods, etc. where he could not see the water, and I would follow him with the stick. When he came to the water, if he stopped, I pounced on him, gave him a whack, and sent him from that point into the water. It soon developed that Tar would get into whatever water he came to if it was on line to his objective. As his training progressed, I worked on various difficult water patterns. One consisted of swimming down a 400 by 20 yard channel. At the end of the channel, it opened out into a large pond of several acres with another 100 yards or so to the far shore, which was the base of the Jamestown Reservoir Dam. This was about 1961 and distances that great were not common in trials. I trained Tar to swim the entire channel, then cross the last piece of water to a dummy. On some days, I placed a dummy on the side of the channel, stopped him in mid-channel, then cast him to the dummy. Then I would bring him back (by water of course) and send him down the channel for the long retrieve. After about two months, he learned to do the routine perfectly without popping, cheating, or no-goes, so I went on to other things and never returned to that spot with him.

That winter I trained in other channels below the dam. Due to the relatively warm water let out by the dam, I trained in all weather, even some days when the temperature was below zero. I would not do this today, being much less hard-nosed than I was then, but it wasn't as rough on the dog as one might think. When Tar came out of the water and that subzero air hit him, the water on his coat would instantly turn to little balls of ice. He would shake off promptly and be quite dry. I often took Tar in the house for a good warm up and a hearty feeding following those afternoons.

The field trials I entered in those days were insignificant affairs compared to what we have now, but they meant a lot to me. They were so-called "club" or "picnic trials" that carried no championship points and only had a dozen or so dogs competing. By the time Tar was a Derby dog of a little over a year of age, I was able to compete with him in the club Open All-Age stakes as well, winning both stakes a majority of the time. On the way home from these trials, I would stop at a Dairy Queen and buy Tar the largest cone available as a reward for his winnings. He would sit on the front seat and politely lick his ice cream as we headed back across the prairie for home. Tar made me feel successful as a trainer, and gave me the idea that I could train a dog to win in more important competitions.

The culminating success of Tar's life, however, was not in field trials, although I have always felt that had I not been a poor art professor at an even more impoverished small college, he could have made his field championship. It was in the hunting field.

One demonstration of Tar's excellence as a duck dog always stands out in my memory. My hunting partner and I were returning home across Spiritwood Lake on a very cold and windy North Dakota day. Ice from the spray was forming on everything in the boat, including its occupants. The waves were big, gray, ominous two-footers, and I had trepidations concerning the seaworthiness of my little boat with its heavy cargo. Midway across the lake, Tar bailed out over the side for no reason that I could ascertain, and started swimming away from the boat. We searched the water to see what he was after, and for a few minutes saw nothing. We cut the motor and were drifting when we saw Tar headed for what looked like a shark's fin sticking up in the water. The waves were so high that this object was out of sight most of the time. Tar continued his pursuit and finally overtook his object, put his head under water, and came up with a fine Canada goose. Someone had apparently shot this goose, broken a wing, and been unable to make the retrieve.

Tar came back with the goose with a tremendous look of satisfaction, although I am sure not to exceed what I felt. We pulled the starter cord on the little Johnson 2.5, and continued across the windswept lake. We didn't notice the wind, though, nor the icy spray, or the rough water. My dog had done something wonderful. We were warm.

CHAPTER 4

PUPPY OBEDIENCE

THE PURPOSE OF OBEDIENCE WORK with a young puppy (under six months) is to develop his responsiveness to you as his trainer, and his willingness to learn. Performance of the commands is of lesser importance. While most puppies learn fast and may become quite polished in their obedience work, we recommend that you not go out of your way to enforce reliability beyond the practice and repetition we describe in this chapter. A puppy has many things to learn, some of which may be inhibited by too much responsibility. Remember our goals: confidence, initiative, and retrieving desire as well as responsiveness to training.

Variations in personality emerge in puppyhood, and each presents its own challenges in training. Some puppies are naturally "dominant," with less-than-usual inclination to take direction. These often show a lot of mounting behavior as puppies and may start lifting their legs as early as three months. Some are simply independent; they may range out far from you on walks, not return well on retrieves, etc. Other puppies may be excessively dependent or lacking in confidence. All of these puppies, and those with other personalities as well, are made much more trainable and pleasant to work with by a good course in puppy obedience, or "learning how to learn." With the dominant-acting puppy in particular, we do not recommend any harsh restraints or confrontational procedures such as pinning the pup on his back. Establishing your leadership by patiently teaching him to respond to your commands is far more effective. With the timid puppy, be careful not to reward fearful behavior by petting or "encouraging" him. Better to ignore such displays, matter-of-factly maintain your standards for commands, and praise the puppy for compliance.

Since your puppy's attitude is our primary concern, we recommend that you focus on your teaching procedures, and let the results come as they will. One popular way of saying this today is to take a "process-oriented" approach rather than a "goal-oriented" one. Concentrate on making each training session as effective as you can, and chances are you'll be amazed at how quickly your puppy learns. One of the most important things you can do is extremely easy — set aside five minutes every day and devote it to training your puppy. Consistent sessions of this kind not only make for very rapid learning, but they contribute greatly to your puppy's confidence in you.

Puppies change rapidly as they grow. One day a certain obedience routine may be too much for a puppy. A few days or a couple of weeks later, the same puppy might learn the routine quickly with no accompanying setbacks. Be sure to keep your training sessions short, and be on the lookout for signs that your puppy may not be ready for what you are teaching. Signs include an apparent decrease in enthusiasm for retrieving, less-than-normal inclination to return on a retrieve, an increase in submissive behavior (ears down, lying down, acting "clingy" and staying close to your feet), and possibly a decreased enthusiasm for coming to you. Any of these changes may occur spontaneously as your pup grows and changes, of course, but if you are in doubt about a procedure, especially if your pup's eagerness to retrieve slackens, ease up and do something else for a while.

The Sit and Release Commands

Teaching sit may begin as early as you like, although we recommend letting your puppy settle in for at least a day or two after you bring him home. You can introduce praise ("Good boy!") and a release command at the same time. Remember, your puppy does not yet understand that you want to train him, or even that you plan to exert some influence on how he behaves. He will only understand what you teach him.

To introduce sit, start by getting on the puppy's level. You can sit on the floor or lift the puppy onto a table if you like. Place one hand on his chest and the other on his rear end just in

Gently "collapse" your puppy into a sitting position, as described in the text.

front of his tail. Pronounce the word, "Sit" as you gently collapse the puppy into a sitting position. Immediately say, "Good!" in a warm, encouraging voice. Stroke your puppy's head and neck as you do. Then, give your release command, which can be "OK," "Hie on," or whatever you choose, and let him go. This should all happen fairly quickly. Our expectation is modest — that your puppy will associate the word "sit" with assuming the sitting position. Holding him forcibly in the position is counterproductive.

Repeat this sequence several times. Repetition is the key to learning for a very young puppy. Most likely, after a few repetitions, your puppy will remain in position after you give the release command. Perhaps this won't happen in the first session, but it probably will at some point. Pat your puppy in the side of the ribcage while saying, "Hie on" in an excited tone of voice. If this doesn't get him up, lift him gently with both hands around the ribcage/belly area and give another pat on the side. Allow him some time to wriggle, sniff around, and so forth before repeating the sit routine.

The release command is as important as any other your dog will learn. A dog needs to understand when he is under command and when that responsibility is over. This will become more obvious when you start working on commands that have some duration, such as stay and heel. Every stay or heel command must end with a release or another command. If your dog is left to decide for himself when an exercise is over, he will obey for only a short while until his attention wanders, then progress to increasingly erratic performance.

Up to about ten repetitions of the sit routine are enough for one session. Quit sooner if you like; sometimes a puppy gets obviously bored with this procedure. You can work on teaching sit three or four times a day if you are so inclined — it is something constructive that you can do during your puppy's play sessions in the house. Sometimes your puppy will seem fairly cooperative, while at other times he may seem almost impossible. Suspend sessions when your puppy is in an "impossible" mood (with wild hand-biting, struggling, etc.). He will learn more effectively when in a cooperative mood, and as his training advances, will be in such a mood more of the time.

We like to leave the other formal commands until the puppy is about four months old, but it is useful to work on getting your puppy to come to you when his name is called. Little puppies are usually sociable. If your pup has already checked out the new sights and smells in an area, it is pretty easy to attract him to you. Call his name, clap your hands, run away (but don't outrun your puppy), and as he approaches, crouch down and spread your arms open wide. Praise him, pet him, and generally make a fuss over him when he gets to you. It is important never to punish your puppy in any way after you call him and he comes to you. If you think he deserves punishment for something, too bad. He will connect any punishment with the act of coming to you, and will be less eager to come in the future.

When your puppy reaches about four months of age, you can begin to work on additional obedience commands. We feel the fastest and least stressful learning is accomplished when both praise and correction are used.

When possible, we try to teach by demonstrating an exercise, using praise to help make it clear what is desired, and introducing corrections only after several practice sessions when the puppy has had plenty of opportunity to learn what we want. Keep in mind that your puppy is still learning how to learn — he will slowly come to understand the training relationship, and that you want him to do certain things. This early in his life, though, he doesn't grasp that you have in mind a set of rules for him to live by — so if he disobeys, don't get angry at him. Just keep teaching the exercises as clearly and patiently as you can.

A Few Words About Praise

You will need to find the level of praise that works best for your puppy. Praise may be verbal ("Good boy!" or "Attagirl!") or physical (anything from a pat to a vigorous ear-scratch or neck-rub). We find, in general, Chesapeakes thrive on plenty of praise, which functions both to let them know when they are doing something right, and as reward. The majority of Labrador and golden retrievers, however, must be praised in a more subdued manner, as individuals of these breeds often take enthusiasm as an invitation to stop concentrating. Many Lab and golden puppies cannot be touched at all without "breaking," i.e. forgetting all about training. It is worthwhile to try, as you proceed with puppy obedience, to teach your puppy to remain in position while you touch him gently around the ears. Verbal praise can also break a dog's concentration, so watch your puppy's response and moderate your tone, duration, and enthusiasm level.

It is possible to over-praise a dog even if he does not "break" from position. This is a common mistake of novice trainers. The appearance is of "trying too hard" to reward a dog's action, repeating "Good dog, GOOD dog," while rubbing the dog up enthusiastically. It is as if the handler lacks confidence his or her praise can be effective — in fact, such excessive praise becomes meaningless to the dog in short order. Remember, timing is important. A single, businesslike "Good dog," with or without a touch to the ears, coinciding with or immediately following a dog's action, is more effective, and less distracting, than a drawn-out session of excessive praise.

With puppies, we use lighter correction than we do for older dogs. The purpose of a correction at this stage is to interrupt whatever your puppy is doing and get his attention so you can get him into position to earn praise. At the age of four months, your puppy can wear a chain training collar or "choke chain" during training. Be sure to put it on correctly as shown in Chapter 1.

The Heel Command

Start by getting your puppy into position, seated by your left side, facing forward. Heeling on the left is the usual practice (required in competition obedience); if you would prefer your dog to heel on the right, just reverse right and left in these instructions. The leash must be slack, now and throughout training on heel. If it is taut, your puppy will pull against it, trying to get out of position instead of learning to stay in it. Say, "Mike, heel," as you step forward with your left foot. Praise your puppy

Starting position for heeling. Note slack in the lead.

if he gets to his feet and moves along with you. The trick is to teach the puppy that you want him to stay on your left side, without being too hard on him in the process. Continue moving briskly forward; this will help keep your puppy's attention on you. At first, you just want to get him walking on your left without pulling at the leash (forward, back, or sideways) or crossing to the other side. When he gets far out of position (more than three or four feet), give a couple of quick jerks back toward the proper position as you repeat, "Heel." Do not pull him back. Praise him as he approaches the desired position at your side.

With many puppies, the number of corrective jerks of the lead can be reduced by using a training stick, held in the right hand, to help keep the puppy in position. Usually the stick is held so the end is in front of the puppy's nose, preventing him

Moving briskly helps hold your puppy's attention and reduces the need for correction.

from forging ahead; you can also hold it to your right and angled backward to keep your puppy from crossing behind you.

After your puppy has strayed from position, been corrected back and praised three or four times, both of you are due for a break. When your puppy is approximately in position by your left side, stop walking and tell him to "sit." In the confusion of trying to figure out this new exercise, your puppy may not sit immediately, so be prepared to back up your command gently but firmly. Grasp the leash near the clip with your right hand and pull upward while you place your left hand on your puppy's hindquarters and press down. Praise as soon as he is seated.

Pause for a few seconds, then start again. Be sure to give the "Heel" command just as you begin your first step forward. Continue to use multiple quick jerks when he strays, and praise him when he is in the approximate position. Stop frequently, enforcing the sit command gently as needed.

Most puppies learn in a session or two that they are to move along with you on the heel command, and stop when you stop. Comprehending the idea of maintaining position takes a little longer. Although most novice trainers tend to adjust to the puppy, slowing down when the puppy lags and speeding up when he forges ahead, we find that pups learn heeling faster when we do the opposite. Instead of accommodating your puppy, exaggerate his errors and correct. If he lags, break into a run, repeat "Heel," and give several quick jerks to make him catch up to you. When he forges ahead, slow down and correct if he doesn't promptly slow to stay with you. If he drifts far to the left, take a quick step to the right and correct. Remember to praise as he comes back into position.

If your puppy crosses over to the wrong side, tell him "No" and use a series of jerks to get him back to your left. To keep from getting the leash tangled around your legs, it may help to turn —

to the right if your puppy drifted across in front of you, or to the left if he crossed behind you — as you correct.

To help your puppy learn quickly with as little correction as possible, keep the first heeling sessions simple. Move in a straight line (except as suggested above), and do not insist on too high a standard — correct only when he is well out of position. In addition, keep the first lessons particularly short. Two or three minutes is plenty. There is a point in a training session where more work only detracts from the dog's learning. For young puppies learning to heel, this point is reached quickly! Finish the training session with a retrieve or two if your puppy will return to you; you can even reward him by allowing him to carry the dummy all the way back to the house, if he will carry without dropping.

Many field-trialers nowadays are training "two-sided" dogs, who can heel on either the left or the right. In field-trial marking tests, the dog is sent from the right or left side as a cue that he should go on that side of a gun station, or because the line to a blind is easier to get from that side. This is purely a competitive device. If your main interest is hunting, we recommend you train your dog to stay on one side or the other simply because one-sided heeling is simpler to learn, and we want your puppy's introduction to obedience training to be as uncomplicated as possible.

Once your puppy begins to catch on to heeling, you can make the exercise more interesting by incorporating turns as well as changes of pace. The easiest turn is a right turn. Pivot on your left foot, step out quickly on your right and, depending on whether your puppy is paying attention or not, he will either keep up with you (earning your praise) or get jerked. You can also turn 180° to the right, reversing direction. Most puppies enjoy the game of trying to keep up and avoid being caught off-guard. On left turns, shorten the leash so you will not turn behind your puppy. Don't worry if you bump him with your knee — he will learn to adjust and stay with you. Changing your pace, going faster and slower than normal, will also help keep him paying attention and enjoying the exercise.

Soon your puppy should begin sitting without the reinforcement of your hand on his rear end. When this happens, you know he has an understanding of what "Sit" means, and you can start correcting the sit. Now when you stop, say "Sit" and give a sharp upward jerk on the leash if he does not do so promptly. As your puppy starts to appear confident, and responds to corrections and changes of pace as though he understands, you can increase the length of training sessions to five minutes.

The Stay Command

The next command we teach is stay. With the heel command, your puppy moves as you move; stay will let him know that he is to remain in place as you move. After practicing heel for several days, he will expect to accompany you, so don't expect instant comprehension. When you reach a stopping point and your puppy sits, praise him. Then say the word "Stay" while applying a light upward pull to the leash, and step out in front of your puppy so you are facing him "nose to knees."

At first, require only that your puppy remain sitting while you step in front of him. Step back by his side, praise, and heel forward again. When you reach another stopping point, practice the stay again. Most likely, your pup will stay for five seconds, and you may be able to work up to ten in the first session.

The upward pull on the leash helps your puppy do the right thing and earn your praise. Dogs generally resist a steady pull. If you pull upward gently on the leash as you step out in front, your puppy's natural tendency to resist that pull will lead him to remain in position. If, however, he stands up and/or moves, calmly say "No" and place him back in position. Then step back

Upward tension on the lead tends to make a puppy stay in place.

beside him, praise him, and heel forward again. Do not prolong the stay after your puppy makes an error — place him back and praise him, and the contrast between "wrong" and "right" will be made as clear as possible.

When your puppy can stay for ten seconds with few mistakes, you can try standing a foot away, maintaining the upward pressure on the lead. Next, try releasing the upward pressure briefly, and practice until your puppy will stay for ten seconds with you standing a foot in front of him without tension on the leash. Gradually work up to thirty seconds, and back up to a leash-length away. As your puppy shows that he understands and will not get up the moment he hears your voice, begin praising him every time he looks at you. With repetition, he will develop the habit of paying attention to you while sitting facing you.

Some people prefer to dispense with the "Stay" command and extend the meaning of the word "sit" to mean "sit and stay." In

Work until your puppy will stay at least thirty seconds with the lead slack.

our experience, puppies seem to learn more easily when we teach the command "Stay" separate from "Sit." "Stay" can also be useful in other circumstances — when opening the dog's crate to get a food dish, in teaching steadiness, etc. It is easy enough later to combine the two so that "Sit" means "sit and stay until released." Some of the old-time trainers used only four commands: "heel" (incorporating "here"), "sit" (incorporating "stay"), "back," and "over." Don't forget to end every "stay" command with either a release command or another command such as "Heel."

The Here Command

The here command may be taught from the sit-stay, or by using a helper to restrain your puppy while you walk away and call him. We recommend, however, that you not begin work on here until your puppy understands stay. Once your puppy gets the idea that you may call him to you, he is apt to want to come with you, and to act stressed when you try to make him stay in place.

Learning the stay command first is easier. As you advance, continue practicing stay, or the work on the contradictory here command will make your puppy forget it.

Introducing the here command is easy. Place your puppy on a sit-stay, walk out in front to the length of the leash, say "Mike, here," and guide him to you with the leash. Taking a few steps backward will help him get the idea, and make him come more quickly. Praise him enthusiastically and guide him into a sitting position in front of you. Practice six or eight times in a training session. Don't be too predictable or he will anticipate your command instead of listening for it. Sometimes require him to hold his stay for up to thirty seconds (or more) before calling him, and at other times, call him after a shorter length of time, or return to his side without calling him. Review heeling in between the sit-stay and here commands. Practicing exercises your puppy knows enhances his confidence and his attitude toward the new commands he is learning. In addition, while young dogs learn rapidly, they also unlearn rapidly if the training is not kept up.

If your puppy comes to you before you give the "Here" command, take him back to where he was sitting and gently push him back into position. It is incorrect for him to break his stay without a command, but he is learning to negotiate contradictory commands, so enforcement should be mild. Make him stay briefly, then return to him and heel forward (even if you had planned to call him to you).

Once your puppy understands that "here" is an invitation to break from his stay and run to you, you can begin working on sit-stays and recalls at greater distances. Use a long line attached to your puppy's collar and gradually work at increased distance. Remember to vary the delay before calling him, and include some sit-stays on which you return to his side without calling. As your puppy starts to form the habit of sitting in front when he comes to you, you can begin to tell him to "sit" as he comes in, and delay your praise until he does.

If you have someone to help you train, you can work at greater distances right from the start. Attach a long line to your puppy's choke collar, and a short check cord to his flat collar. Have your assistant hold the short cord as you walk away, making sure your long line does not get tangled around the short cord or your puppy's feet. Your assistant should not pet or talk to your puppy, or give him any commands. His or her job is simply to prevent your puppy from following you. Face your puppy from fifteen or twenty feet away, call him ("Mike, here!"), and use the long line to guide him to you. Praise and make him sit as described above. If your puppy comes to you smoothly, increase the distance. Practice about five or six times in a session, then review heel, sit, and stay for the rest of the five minutes.

You will probably be gratified by your puppy's response to these early coming-when-called exercises. Do not, however, call him when you do not have the means to immediately enforce the command. He is likely to disobey in a less formal setting, and doing so will serve to teach him that he may ignore the here command.

Whistle Commands

We use the whistle because the sound carries well, making it unnecessary to shout when a dog is far away. The standard whistle command for sit is one short blast. While heeling, blow the sit whistle, immediately say, "Sit," and correct your puppy with a quick jerk if he doesn't sit promptly. After a few repetitions, you can leave out the verbal "Sit."

The command for here is several short blasts (two or more). Practice recalls with the whistle first, followed immediately by the command "Here," and a quick jerk on the line toward you if necessary. Praise when your puppy comes to you, as usual. Soon your puppy will come when you whistle.

Returning to Heel Position

Throughout your puppy's training, you will teach a command in one very limited circumstance, then proceed to expand the meaning of the command. With stay, for instance, you started by requiring your pup to remain sitting while you pivoted in front of him briefly, and worked up to asking him to remain in place while you walked twenty or more feet away and stood for thirty seconds or more. Now it is time to expand the meaning of heel from "come along with me, staying at my left side," to include "return to my left side from somewhere else."

In competition obedience, this exercise is called the "finish," and the custom is for the dog to walk around behind the handler to reach the heel position. This is easy for the dog to learn and

"Heeling backwards." At first, your puppy will probably need encouragement to follow on your left side.

some dogs (particularly many Chesapeakes) have a strong tendency to return this way even after being taught otherwise. In retriever work, however, we want the dog to make a beeline for our left side, turn in place, and sit without walking behind us. Dogs that are taught to walk behind the handler may try to take refuge there when the work starts to become challenging. In addition, when a handler is lining a dog up on a blind retrieve and needs to direct his attention further to the left, the handler turns left toward the dog and says, "Heel." The handler expects the dog to turn to his left and sit facing the new direction, but a dog trained to walk around his handler may well get up, walk in a circle around the handler, and sit back down, still inaccurately positioned.

A good way to begin teaching your puppy to return to the heel position is to begin with him sitting facing you (as on the sit-stay). Take the leash in your left hand and say, "Heel," as you begin walking backward. Most likely your pup will want to follow you on your right — this maintains the familiar pattern in which you are on his right. Guide him to your left with the leash, and pat your left thigh with your right hand to attract his attention to that side. A heeling stick extended to your right can help convey that your left side is the place to be.

When your puppy starts to follow on your left side, praise him. Continue a couple more steps, then start walking forward, returning along the same route, and repeat "Heel." Your puppy should turn toward you and heel properly forward at your left side. If he tries to turn away from you, make sure that when you repeat the exercise, you step to your right before moving forward. This makes turning toward you pretty obvious to your puppy.

Some puppies learn this quickly and, after a couple of sessions, will come to the heel position, turn and sit with only a minor cue consisting of a step back on the left foot and a gesture to the side with the left hand, followed by returning the left foot to its place. Others find returning to heel a real stumbling block. Additional practice at heeling as you walk forward and backward, and change direction, helps clarify the problem and is good preparation for teaching your dog to take a line later in training.

Words to the Wise
In an effort to achieve finished results at an early age, many owners want to have their puppies steady, perfect in obedience, and doing a number of drills at a very early age. Part of the reason this trend has caught hold is that puppies are, indeed, capable of being trained to a high degree of reliability. Another reason, we suspect, is the natural competitiveness of dog owners, wanting to have the best, brightest, quickest-learning dog. Our experience with dogs raised this way, however, is that their ultimate capabilities are limited — probably because the one-sided emphasis on control adversely affects development of initiative, confidence, and desire.

This concludes the list of obedience exercises we recommend for puppies under the age of six months. While a few puppies are precocious and can learn more exercises without any apparent cost to their confidence and enthusiasm, these are a small minority. These precocious puppies will not suffer from a conservative approach to training. The purpose of training at this stage is to develop an attitude of willingness and an orientation to learning from the trainer. The payoff for careful, patient work during puppyhood will be lifelong, making training easier and more pleasant, and making your life with your dog more harmonious. Do not sacrifice these benefits in pursuit of perfect obedience or the appearance of rapid progress. Stick to the exercises and degree of reliability described in this chapter, and you will achieve the goal of nurturing a good attitude toward further training.

REAL DOGS

PUPPY ANECDOTES

by John

PUPPIES ARE AN UNPREDICTABLE LOT. Those of us who have bought and raised a number of puppies realize that the early traits shown by various puppies frequently have little relationship to those we see when the dog is full grown. These surprises come frequently enough to make unpredictability the rule, rather than the exception.

Often, the slow puppy turns out fast. The most notable example of this in my memory is FC Shake 'N Jake III, who at four months was one of the slowest puppies I have ever seen. Ed Forry, his owner, and I agreed it would probably be best to give Jake away, but even then Jake was an excellent marker. As Jake grew up, he became one of the fastest retrievers I have seen and made an outstanding field trial dog.

On the opposite side of the coin, I have had a large number of pups that showed great speed and enthusiasm when small but turned out to be slow and lethargic adults. Some of this, of course, can be brought on by incorrect training, but some of it also just happens.

An aggressive attitude toward water is something we all love to see in a puppy, and yet the puppy who shows the greatest inclination to get wet is often the most difficult to train in precise water work, particularly if the love of water takes the form of aimless, and seemingly endless, play in the water (water freaking). The water freaking syndrome is particularly common in the Chesapeake breed, and we try to control it early in the dog's life.

Tar of Moon Lake (1965 North Dakota State Open

Champion) and Tarheel Jade, who won a 105-dog Open All-Age stake, both hated water as puppies. Both became, with extensive training, two of the best water blind dogs that I have ever run in field trials, and both were exceptionally strong water dogs while hunting, even in severe weather. Usually the pup that hates the water when young will carry that trait into adulthood even though some aspects of their water work may be acceptable. Both Tar and Jade continued to have a slow water entry throughout their careers, particularly on marks, even though they were very stylish when hunting.

Size is another unknown in judging the future of a puppy. Although the big puppy in a litter will generally turn out to be good-sized, he will usually be surpassed by one of the smaller pups. Often the large puppy will reach a medium size rather quickly, achieve an early maturity, and remain at that stature. Other individuals seem to start out fairly small and continue growing long past their littermates' maturity to become large. I try to avoid retrievers of great size because of various health problems and lack of longevity, common in oversized dogs. At one time, when I had Chesapeakes exclusively, most of the puppies I raised matured at 100 pounds or more, even though their parents were medium 70- to 80-pound dogs. My first Chesapeake, though, Rum River Buck, was sired by a 120-pound dog, and he turned out to be an 80-pounder. I later realized smaller size was a plus.

The training a puppy receives is usually an indicator of how he or she will turn out. With some frequency, however, methods of training that are generally advised against will yield amazing results. We consistently recommend short but frequent training sessions. My first registered retriever, a nice golden female I called "Reba," was subjected to repeated lengthy training sessions, most of which would ruin the average prospect. The day I brought

Reba home, at 7 weeks, I put a collar and lead on her and taught her to heel. It was a long and rough session, taking the better part of an afternoon, but she learned the lesson well and turned out to be a rather polished retriever at 11 or 12 months of age, doing small-scale (75 to 100 yard) multiple marks and blind retrieves with precision — although admittedly with some lack of style. Her land blinds were taught on the snowy streets of Minneapolis in mid-winter at 1:30 a.m. — the time I got home from my night job when I was a university student. I would plant dead pigeons in the neighbors' front yards and line her to them, giving hand signals from the middle of the road. The street lights reflecting off the snow gave us plenty of light. This was in 1952.

Puppies are fun, especially when they are cute and energetic, which most of the good ones are. Pudge, FC Oakhill Exponent, was such a puppy, as was her littermate, FC-AFC A. P. Charlie. Pudge possessed boundless energy and a love for what you wanted her to do.

From early puppyhood, Pudge never tolerated being held. She was well built and strong enough to wrestle her way out of any hold I tried in an attempt to contain her. As an adult, she retained this ability to get away from physical restraint and correction. If she was on a lead and I tried to strike her with the training stick, she could quickly dodge my efforts. This made it particularly hard to establish line manners and steadiness as I could not guide her or reinforce commands with the stick.

Pudge also despised drills such as mowed yard patterns with multiple dummies at different stations. As a result, I had to do almost all of her early blind training in the field on fresh ground.

She was an extremely hard-going water dog, but she often viewed the water as an obstacle to circumvent in the interest of speed. As a result, she showed a strong inclination to "cheat the water." When she discovered through training that I wouldn't tolerate cheating, she quickly became one of the most direct and fastest water dogs I have trained.

As a puppy, Pudge showed indications of being a proficient marker, yet when more than one thrower was stationed in the field, she became confused as to which mark she was supposed to retrieve. This resulted in a lot of popping on multiple marks. The problem was solved later in her life at about three-and-a-half years of age by a repetition of "forcing on back." At that time, her mind seemed to magically clear and her marking problems largely disappeared. Pudge went on to become a very good field trial performer.

We like puppies that show "all the right stuff" from birth on. This doesn't happen often, though. Puppy-rearing is fraught with reversals and advancements that are impossible to predict. We can only trust to the breeding we have chosen, train as well as we can, and hope for the best.

CHAPTER 5

FORMAL OBEDIENCE

I N FORMAL OBEDIENCE, WE TEACH A DOG to respond reliably to commands the first time they are given. Our demands are greater than in puppy training; we use corrections more freely and we require the dog to take responsibility for "getting it right." This training requires a certain degree of maturity on the part of the dog. Accordingly, we recommend waiting to begin formal obedience until your puppy is about six months old. Do not, however, assume that because your puppy is growing up, you can disregard the attitude you have carefully fostered in puppy work. Your dog's attitude must have primary consideration throughout training. In formal obedience, a good attitude is maintained by making sure your dog understands what is expected before correcting; by correcting decisively and with good timing when appropriate; and by making sure your requirements and responses are as consistent as possible.

In addition, of course, it is important to continue to limit the duration of your training sessions. Do not exceed ten minutes. Your dog's attention span may appear to last considerably longer, but learning and retention will be much better with short sessions. Do, however, train consistently, six days a week if possible.

Progress in obedience work can be significantly enhanced by the manner in which you fit it into your dog's daily routine. If your dog has been alone and idle in her crate for a couple of hours when training begins, she will be attentive and inclined to view the training session as a pleasant change. If, however, you call her in from playing with the neighborhood children to insist that she sit, stay, and otherwise exert self-discipline, she may view the training as drudgery. For the sakes of her attitude and her progress, therefore, plan your training session to follow a session in the crate.

Make sure your dog is wearing a properly fitted chain training collar or "choke chain," described in Chapter 1. If you will use an e-collar to train your dog, put it (or the dummy collar if you have one) on your dog every time you get her out for a training session. Adjust the e-collar to ride high on your dog's neck behind her head. Leave the transmitter in the box, and plan not to shock your dog until she has worn the collar for at least two weeks, preferably a month. Remove the e-collar when a session is over.

Praise continues to be an important tool in formal obedience training. In formal obedience, praise your dog when she executes a command properly without a correction, and praise her when she gives the appropriate response following a correction. If your dog crosses behind you while heeling, for example, correct her back to proper position and tell her, "Good dog" as soon as she is in position. Praising immediately after a correction is unnatural for many people, but identifying the correct response regardless of whether correction was needed is good dog training.

Reinforcement of Sit, Heel, and Stay

While we held off on the corrections and on our demands of your puppy prior to six months of age, now we expect more. Our goal is perfect responsiveness and reliability, so once you have given your dog a fair chance to understand what you require, correct decisively for any failures or slow responses. If your dog is slow or reluctant to sit, give a quick upward jerk with the lead (you can do this effectively using both hands, propelling your dog into a sit) or alternatively, give her a sharp whack on the hindquarters with the heeling stick. Continue correcting on sit until your dog plops her rear end down sharply when you come to a halt.

A working retriever should sit squarely and symmetrically, not slouched over on one haunch. It is common for puppies to sit sloppily, however, and many of them will outgrow this without any correction. If your dog persists with sloppy sits, straighten him up with a nudge of the foot or an upward pull on the lead, but not harshly, while repeating "Sit." Be consistent in your requirement of proper sit position, and your dog will eventually sit properly without enforcement.

If you have not yet broken your dog of forging ahead and pulling at the lead, now is the time to do so. A dog that is constantly out in front is generally unheedful, and may be difficult to line up on blind retrieves later, to say nothing of the inconvenience of constant pulling whenever you take her for walks on lead. The key to solving this problem is to maintain slack in the lead. Slip the hand-loop of your six-foot lead over your right hand, and also loop the lead so you grasp it near its middle with the same hand. When your dog is in proper heeling position, this should allow three feet of lead to fall slack between your hand and your dog.

Tell your dog to "Heel" as you step forward. Any time she gets out in front of you where she can potentially tighten the lead, turn quickly (to your right) and head in the opposite direction before she can do so. If your dog is heedless, she will receive a jolt — and she will quickly learn she had better keep back where she can pay better attention. Commit yourself to keeping the lead slack from now on. When a lead is taut, you broadcast your intentions and your dog has no need to concentrate.

A dog that is sniffing the ground is inattentive, so do not allow this behavior when she is under command. Depending on your preference and your coordination, you can correct this either by swatting your dog's nose with the stick or by jerking her head up using the lead while saying "Heel!" This can be a challenge as many dogs become proficient at the "quick sniff," so you have little warning until the sniff is over and it is hard to catch your dog in the act. Persist, however, and soon your dog will heel properly at your side with her head up.

Your corrections should be firm and emphatic and should make an impression. While ground-sniffing requires more repetition than most infractions, you should see improvement in sitting response, heeling position, and other areas after two or three corrections. If you are making solid leash corrections with both hands and your dog continues to act unresponsive, try switching to a pinch collar. Chances are your dog's response after two or three corrections will be a pleasant surprise. Do not, however, leave a pinch collar on your dog when you are not training.

Leash-jerks may be used in a similar manner to improve reliability on the sit-stay. Instead of simply placing her back in position, begin giving your dog a correction (step in and jerk upward on the leash) when she breaks her stay. The rate at which you attempt to progress will influence your dog's number of mistakes and the corrections she receives. In consideration of your dog's all-important attitude, advance at a rate that allows her to be successful, holding the stay until your return, at least 80 percent of the time. After a correction, return to your dog's side and praise her.

In order to make use of the commands in daily life, you must "proof" each exercise. Practice, with corrections as needed, around progressively stronger distractions. Useful distractions include a cage containing a small animal, people, an open car door, unfamiliar scents, a new location, and people engaged in activity. An obedience class also provides a strongly distracting environment in which to work.

Your dog's potential reliability is limited only by the limits to your follow-through. Remember, though, that until your dog is dependable, you must never give a command that you are not in a position to enforce. If your dog fails to comply and goes uncorrected, much work will be undone.

Finally — Reliably Coming When Called

When your dog is responding favorably to your increased requirements for reliability and attentiveness on *heel, sit,* and *stay,* she is ready to begin learning to come reliably when called. Devote one training session to practicing the here command as described in Chapter 4. When you are sure she remembers and understands what "Here" means, at least when she is on the long check cord, start giving a solid jerk on the cord as you call her whether you are working from a sit-stay or using a helper. Insist that she sit when she comes to you. As with all other commands, execution of here must have a definite conclusion. Sitting in front of you is definite; returning to your general vicinity is not. Your dog should remain sitting until you release her or give her another command.

Getting a reliable recall is one of the areas where the e-collar can be a big help. If you are using an e-collar, follow the procedure for collar conditioning (see page 116), after which you will use the collar to reinforce coming when called.

If you are not using an e-collar, use your helper to simulate a refusal on the part of your dog, for which you will then correct. Have your helper hold a lead or check cord attached to your dog's flat collar as before. You will walk away to the full length of your long check cord, which is attached to the chain collar or pinch collar. Wait from 10 to 30 seconds, then call your dog. Your helper should be previously instructed not to let go of the lead until you signal. Since your dog cannot come to you, give a solid jerk on the long check cord, repeating "Molly, here!" and signal your helper to release your dog.

Repeat this drill six to eight times in a session. Sometimes signal your helper to release your dog on the first command, so she can come to you and be praised. Other times, delay your signal so you can get in one or even two solid corrections. If your dog runs towards you but then sweeps by, step on the cord and repeat "Here" just as she feels the pull. Pick up the cord if necessary, reel her in, and make her sit.

If you do not have a helper, you can get the same effect using two long check cords, one of which you loop around a tree or other stationary object. Then hold both the line that restrains your dog and the line with which you correct your dog. Instead of signaling your helper, release your dog when you choose.

After three or four sessions, start testing your dog's responsiveness. Have the cord already laid out on the ground as you walk away from her, so that she can clearly see you are not carrying it and do not have a hold on it when you face her and call her. In this situation, have your helper release your dog if she moves to respond to your first command. If your dog ignores you because you are not holding the long line, have your helper keep his or her hold on the other cord while you pick up your line and give a solid correction. If you are manipulating two ropes, you can restrain your dog unobtrusively with a foot on the cord that holds her back.

If your dog fails this test, keep practicing for a couple more sessions until she doesn't take the absence of a cord in your hand as an excuse for not responding. Then expand on the "no hands" setup. Walk out past the end of your long line and call the dog. Again, if she responds, she should be immediately released to come to you. If she refuses, have your helper restrain her long enough for you to correct.

When your dog's responses to the here command have been impeccable for at least two training sessions of 6 - 8 repetitions each, it is time to take the command to a less-formal setting. Put a medium-length check cord (20 feet or so) on your dog's training collar and let your dog drag it as you walk casually into your training area. Encourage your dog to relax and explore. Wait for her to get some distance from you and call her. Most dogs will respond perfectly. If yours does not, approach her calmly until you can step on the cord. Pick up the cord and give a couple of sharp yanks, repeating, "Here!" then walk to the spot where you initially called, and make her come all the way in and sit in front of you. Release her and wait for another opportunity to call her. It may take a while for her to drift away from you — it is better not to call immediately when she does, or she will probably start sticking by your side. Wait a minute or two to let her get involved in her explorations, then call.

When you are getting consistently good responses in this casual situation, you can continue with yard and field work with your dog dragging a check cord. Usually you can switch to a shorter, 5- to 6-foot cord for field work. If you have made a practice of never calling her when you are not in a position to enforce the command, this training will be close to 100 percent effective. Now that your dog has plenty of experience with the here command, you can correct the occasional refusal by going to her, correcting her sharply, and requiring that she return with you to the place from which you called her. If refusals are more than occasional, your dog needs more work on the long line.

Reinforcement with the Electric Collar

If you are using the e-collar to train your dog, you can begin collar-conditioning when she is sitting reliably and heeling confidently without any corrections. "Collar-conditioning" means introducing your dog to the sensation of electric shock from the collar, and making sure that she understands the shock as correction and responds to it by executing the command that is given. For the e-collar to be useful in training, your dog must not fear it or react excitedly to it, so careful introduction is necessary.

We like to introduce the collar on the sit command. As we noted earlier, there are dogs who are very slow to give a reliable response to "Sit." It is mandatory that your dog be responding promptly and reliably on "Sit" before you begin. We use the "continuous" mode for collar-conditioning, so if your collar has a choice of momentary or continuous, set it on continuous.

Many professional trainers work with the highest few settings on the collar from the beginning. We recommend, however, that the novice trainer start with a more modest shock, in the low to medium range. First do some heeling and sitting, holding the leash in your left hand and the transmitter in your right. Now watch your dog closely as you say, "Sit" and press the "low" button on the transmitter (or the single continuous button). Press and release the button in half a second or less; do not keep holding it down until your dog sits. If your dog reacts by cocking an ear, turning her head, or stopping part way into her sit and looking distracted, you know that she felt the shock. Heel forward a little way and repeat. You should press the button as close to giving the command as possible. If your dog is slow to sit, or does not sit, give your standard sit correction. At this point, the shock is more of a distraction than a correction, and needs to be coupled with your conventional enforcement. If you see no reaction at all, you probably need to try the next higher level.

Once you find the right level so that your dog reacts when you press the "low" button, continue practicing heeling and sitting. Do not shock every time on the sit, but do use the brief continuous shock on some of the sits, backing it up with your standard correction if your dog hesitates. Do not press the button more than ten times in a session. You may find your dog lagging or otherwise trying to avoid the heel position; this is normal.

Continue the same pattern in your next training session. Try to be unpredictable about when you will accompany the "Sit" command with shock, or a "nick" as we call it. Mix in an occasional stronger nick. Continue to keep them short, however — less than half a second. If your dog lags, enforce proper heel position firmly but not threateningly. Keep working until your dog's response to "Sit"/nick is to sit promptly, without any lagging or extraneous movement.

Once your dog is responding well to e-collar correction on *sit*, you can begin to use it on *here*. Work with a helper as we described before, or substitute a long line looped around a tree if no helper is available. Call your dog, "Molly, here!" and immediately nick with the collar. Use the long line to give your dog a solid pull in your direction in case the shock makes her hesitate. Practice several recalls in this manner, sometimes including a brief nick, sometimes omitting it. As with *sit*, mix in an occasional medium or high nick, but use mostly the low setting. As before, six to eight recalls in one session is enough.

Before getting rid of the line, we like to follow a "simulated refusal" procedure similar to the one described in the conventional (no e-collar) method. Instruct your helper not to let your dog go until you give a signal. Two or three times in a session, delay your signal long enough to get in a correction — a second nick (and even a third). Time the nick to coincide with, or precede by a split second, your repeat of the "Here" command. Try to have the helper release your dog immediately following the second (or third) "Here" command, so the command provides a "way out" for your dog. Praise your dog as soon as she starts moving toward you, and when she gets to you, make her sit for more praise. Mix these simulated refusals in with instances where you call and nick, and instances where you call, have your helper release your dog, and allow her to complete the recall without a correction.

Many dogs will bolt in an attempt to escape collar pressure. Of course, yours will learn that bolting is no escape. If you can tempt her into bolting with the long line attached, this lesson will be easier than if it is left until later. Try calling her from a distance when an apparent place of "refuge" is close by (in or under a vehicle, or her pen or run). If she bolts, continue to repeat nick/"Here!" nick/"Here!" at about one-second intervals as she runs around trying to escape the shock. If she runs into the "place of refuge," increase the shock to "medium" to help convince her that there is no refuge where she can ignore your command. Continue calling as you go after her and pick up the end of the line. Pull her toward you and, as soon as she is moving, stop calling and nicking, and begin praising her instead. This is a stressful lesson, so give her a chance for an easy repetition of the here command on the line, praise her, and end the session.

When the part-time shock really seems to have sharpened up your dog's response so that she is really digging out to get to you, she is probably ready for the next step. In the next session, use your helper but no long line; otherwise work exactly as before. If your dog comes to you smoothly every time you call, with or without a nick, your collar conditioning is going well. If your dog does not come (perhaps because her short lead caught on something, causing her to stop in confusion) try going to get her and bringing her back to the spot from which you called. If this happens repeatedly, your dog needs more work on the long line.

If your dog bolts at this point, you cannot use the line to help her out of her predicament. If she goes to an area where you are out of her sight, walk to where she can see you. Under stress because of the collar corrections, she is more likely to find the right solution if you make coming to you as easy and obvious as possible. If your dog is properly prepared, she should come to you after exhausting a couple of possibilities for refuge. Praise her and devote the rest of the training session to reviewing things she already knows well. If she bolts on some later occasion, deal with it in the same way. Try to see bolting not as an interruption of your training, but as an opportunity to follow up your training on *here* to make it solid.

Once a dog understands the sit and here commands thoroughly, failures in the field can be addressed using the collar's "momentary" mode (if available on your collar). Resist the temptation to punish your dog with a long, intense shock when she ignores a command. Repeat the command with a momentary nick and in most cases your dog will quickly comply, maintaining her composure and her ability to learn and to concentrate.

Practice the whistle commands for *here* and *sit* with e-collar reinforcement until your dog is thoroughly reliable. If she shows any sign of confusion, couple the whistle commands with verbal commands for a session or two. Blow the whistle (a single blast for *sit*, multiple short blasts for *here*), give the verbal command, and follow up with correction if necessary. After a couple days of practice, you can eliminate the verbal commands.

Sitting at a Distance

Your dog first learned to sit at your side, then to sit in front of you on the recall. A working retriever, however, should sit wherever she is told to sit, not only beside or in front of her master.

This is necessary to the teaching of blind retrieves, of course, but is also useful if you want to position your dog outside of a blind from which you are hunting, and in a variety of other situations. Generalizing the sit command to mean "sit immediately, wherever you are," like other generalizations, cannot be assumed but must be taught.

We begin with a drill called simply the here-sit drill. Usually, we give the commands by whistle, but voice commands work equally well. Sit your dog, tell her to "Stay," and walk away. Whistle her toward you (with the "Here" or come-in whistle), then when she is almost to you, give the sit whistle or say "Sit." Your dog will probably sit right in front of you as she is accustomed to do. Repeat, but this time give the sit whistle when your dog is ten or fifteen feet out, and follow up with a verbal "Sit!" and take a step or two toward her. Fend her off from you with a stick or outstretched foot, repeating "Sit!" if necessary.

Your dog is apt to act confused, since sitting anywhere other than in front of you or at your side does not fall within her understanding of the sit command. If you can get her to sit two feet from you, or even one, praise her — you want her to understand that she is not doing wrong, but doing right. Step forward to her and praise again. Not only are you requiring her to disobey what she thinks "Sit" means, you have prevented her from completing the recall by coming all of the way to you. Going to her at this point seems to defuse some of the tension created by this "double failure." Repeat the entire sequence. It may take some practice until your dog is comfortable sitting one or two feet away, but once you reach that point, you can gradually work for greater distance. The here whistle command is being redefined to mean "come towards me," while the sit command is being expanded to mean "sit where you are." This is demanding and confusing, so be patient and avoid harsh corrections when teaching this drill.

While many dogs find the remote sit initially confusing, some continue to fail to comprehend it. We use a method to reinforce the exercise that is perhaps unique to our training program and is effective and gentle. Attach two ropes of about 30' in length to the dog. Hold the end of one of these ropes and have a helper hold the other, so your dog is between you and cannot run to feither you or your helper. Then walk the dog slowly across the yard, at intervals blowing the sit whistle command followed by the verbal "Sit" command. Most dogs that have been well prepared in basic obedience will pick up this principle and learn to sit promptly at the sound of the whistle. Even the dog with a "hangup" will eventually realize that you are not angry with her failure to come to you, only persistent in requesting her to "Sit," which she will then do.

Other Useful Commands: Down and Kennel

The down command is not used in standard retriever work, but is very useful around the house and in hunting. To teach the *down*, start with your dog sitting at your left side. Kneel by her (bend down if you're limber) and take hold of the leash close to her collar with your left hand. Say, "Down" as you reach behind her right foreleg to take hold of her left, raising her forefeet off the ground and gently lowering her body to the ground (see photo on next page). This maneuver is aided by your left forearm across her shoulders, elbow away from you, hand still holding the leash. Praise immediately when she is in position and allow her to get up. Do some heeling, and repeat.

With most dogs, we just continue with this procedure until the dog starts lying down on her own when we give the command. Commonly, this takes four or five sessions with eight to ten repetitions per session. Sometimes it takes a little longer and we recommend you keep at it patiently for a couple more days. Some dogs,

This method of placing the dog in a "down" creates a minimum of resistance.

however, will not down on command without some correction.

If you have given your dog plenty of opportunity to learn the down command and she still does not lie down when told, then grasp her leash about six inches from her neck, say "Down," and immediately jerk forcefully forward, down, and to the right. The object is to apply enough forward-and-down force to the right foreleg so that it will buckle at the joint and your dog, unsupported, will be forced to lie down.

Once your dog is lying down on command, it is a simple matter to give the "Stay" command to get her to remain in place. Most dogs seem able to generalize "Stay" to this new position quite easily.

Sometimes retrievers lie down in the field when they should be sitting, especially when the training gets to be confusing and/or stressful. To try to minimize this, do no more work on the *down* than you need to achieve good behavior in the house or in the blind.

The last command we consider in this chapter is the kennel

command. It is useful not only to get your dog to go into her crate or run, but also for directing her to get into something unfamiliar, such as a car or boat. We suggested in Chapter 2 that you use the word "Kennel" every time you put your puppy in her crate. Consistent repetition of this cue is all that is required to get most dogs going willingly into their crates on command. Some dogs, however, do not voluntarily comply with the kennel command. If your dog is well on her way to being obedience trained, she is ready to kennel on command. Hold her by the collar in front of the open door to her crate and say, "Kennel," and swat her across the rear with a stick. Repeat "Kennel"/hit "Kennel"/hit until she goes into her crate. Apply this procedure every time you put your dog in her crate, and soon she will "kennel" readily on command.

BUCK

B UCK, "RUM RIVER BUCK," so named after one of my favorite fishing streams in Minnesota, was my first Chesapeake. I had known the breed as a child, and every neighborhood in Minneapolis seemed to have one or two Chesapeakes wandering around keeping things under control. I had always admired the breed's strength and calm resoluteness, as well as their impressive physical presence, which remains a characteristic of many Chesapeakes today. Their detractors always said they were mean, hard to train, and inclined to fight. There may be merit to the last item in that argument. The were, for the most part, excellent duck dogs, reliable and tough, and more than enough watch dog to keep would-be thieves off the premises. For these reasons, I bought Buck as a four-month-old pup in November of 1952.

The $40 I paid for Buck seemed an inordinate outlay at the time, and nothing would do except to make sure that I put a commensurate effort into his training. From day one, I made demands on Buck, and made them stick. Today, I would be less hard-nosed and would cut a puppy more slack in his daily training. By the time Buck was six months old, he was steady, force fetched (in the manner which we understood it then), and delivering ducks or dummies to hand. I carried a dozen cork decoys to a nearby lake every day, and included them as a part of each training session.

We didn't think along the lines that, "This is only a puppy; if he has much wrong with him, I'll wash him out and get another." A puppy was a commitment, and whatever faults he had, you either lived with them or eliminated them through training. Of course, we had very few perfect dogs in those days, but I guess they are none too plentiful today, either.

Buck probably taught me more than I taught him. Training mistakes were something the dog had to live with and learn from. It was common for a dog to receive a good roughing up for an infraction he was unprepared to understand, or to avoid in the future. But try we did, and over a period of a few months, Buck learned most of what he had to know to operate as a useful duck dog.

Except for one or two sessions per week when I trained with a friend, Buck's lessons were with me alone. I walked to all kinds of difficult locations on my limited training grounds, changing the set-up daily, shouted, "Hey! hey!" and threw his marks. I threw up to three marks at a time, then walked back to where Buck was sitting on the "Stay" command. Then I sent him for the marks one at a time. I was unaware that this was difficult, and he became very proficient as a multiple marker.

My blinds were almost all water blinds because I reasoned that if a bird lit on land, I could easily walk over to it and send the dog in to hunt for it from close range. Generally, when I reached my training area, which was a short walk from my house, I would throw a dummy out into the lake in a downwind direction. At first, I sent Buck to pick these up soon after throwing them out, so they were more or less sight blinds. Soon, however, I was able to throw a dummy and let it drift out into the lake, a couple of hundred yards or so. In the meantime, I worked Buck on a marking problem in another area. When he finished that, I returned to the blind that by that time was far out of sight, and lined and handled Buck to the dummy. We used no sophisticated method of yard training to teach handling, but blew the whistle, hollered, and waved our arms around until the dog got the idea. A lot of dogs picked up handling very quickly by these methods. Of course, the e-collar had not been developed at that time.

Buck's first field trial was an event I'll never forget. It was a puppy stake in late winter, and Buck was about seven months old. Everything in Minnesota at that time was still deep in snow. The puppy stake consisted of four series. Each test had a dead pigeon thrown on the packed snow of a plowed road with about a four foot embankment of snow on either side. The first series consisted of a throw about 40 yards down the middle of the road, then 60 yards for the second, 80 yards for the third, and about 100 yards for the fourth and final series. All throws were down the same road, and the sending line was the same for all four retrieves. So far as I could see, Buck did all of his marks perfectly, went out and returned fast, and made me very proud. This was my first field trial, too. I was so pleased with Buck's work that after each series I drove to a nearby phone booth and called home to report that Buck was still in the trial. I probably have never been more pleased with a dog's work. I surely haven't had more fun at a field trial. At the end of the day, the ribbons for the puppy stake were handed out. I got a green (certificate of merit). Other dogs got the places. I guess they did perfectly, too.

Field trialing in those days, at least for me, was done more to keep the dog in shape and to have something to do in the off season, which was about 10 months of the year, than as an end in itself. There were several local clubs around Minneapolis that specialized in monthly picnic trials, informal events with no championship points. We had puppy stakes, Derbies, Qualifyings and Opens, as well as a hunter's special that was kind of an advanced puppy stake for dogs that were steady and delivering to hand. The club picnic trials were a world unto themselves, and we set great store by dogs that performed well in them. Many greats such as NFC Cork of Oakwood Lane and NAFC-FC Yankee Clipper of Reo Raj ran regularly in these events. For most of us, the rarefied atmosphere of licensed field trials was financially out of reach, and well beyond the capabilities of most of our dogs. We were interested in gun dogs much more than field-trial competition.

With Buck's training quite well in hand and the long hot summer logged about halfway through, I was looking forward to the duck season with keen anticipation. We had trained daily, and I had done everything I could think of to prepare to set forth in October with a Grade-A retriever. Man proposes, and God disposes, the best-laid plans, and all of those clichés are true! One day, while I was packing my burlap bag full of decoys and retrieving dummies to Cedar Lake, Buck broke away from his heeling position and went over an embankment out of sight after a rabbit, cat, or something. There was a train going by, and by the time I caught up with Buck he was lying near the tracks with his left front foot badly bloodied up. I got help from home immediately, bound the foot to stay the bleeding, and rushed Buck to the nearest vet. I didn't see the accident, but he had apparently got three-quarters of the main pad pinched off under the wheel of the train with a resulting split in the skin on the top of his foot between the two center toes to an inch or so above the first joint of his foot. The vet didn't know if we could save the foot, but he did his best, stitching and repairing. I took Buck home that day to embark on a six week healing program. This took me well into the duck season, and consisted of cleaning and dressing the wound four times a day.

As Buck's foot healed, it became apparent that it would never be 100 percent functional, as the main pad was forever gone. The area on top of the foot never quite healed over. Still, Buck could move pretty well after a few weeks and I was hoping, once more, to enjoy some of the season's hunting with him.

It was mid-November and things were rapidly icing over when I first took Buck hunting. There were very few ducks to be seen on the mostly iced-over western Minnesota lake where we went. Buck's foot was still in protective bandaging and I was in the midst of my first case of "Asian Flu," with a fever of 103°. We were bemoaning the demise of a nonproductive duck season, the flu, Buck's foot, and other negative topics, when a lone bluebill came by high and fast overhead. I swung my gun, fired, and down it came, sliding across a sheet of glassy ice until it plopped over the edge into the open water.

When Buck saw the duck go down, he broke, took off across the ice, and went over the edge into swimming water about 100 yards out where he overtook his bluebill. With the bandaged front foot, he could not make it back onto the ice, so I stripped down to my long underwear, picked up a stray fence post, and began to beat a path through the ice to him. By the time I reached the open water where Buck was swimming with the duck still in his mouth, I was chest-deep in ice water. The air temperature was about 15° F. Needless to say, we both beat a hasty retreat for shore, and my hunting partner had the car well warmed up when I arrived. I then stripped down to no clothes, wrapped up in a woolen blanket, and got in the heated car.

As soon as I stopped shaking, my body experienced a sudden rush of heat, my skin turned bright red, and I began to feel warm. It wasn't long until I got into dry clothes and became comfortable. The truly amazing thing was that my fever subsided and I experienced no more symptoms of the flu.

Buck and I had a couple of memorable hunts that year on the Mississippi River north of Minneapolis. Buck lived a long and productive life as a hunting retriever with a close friend and hunting companion. I'll never forget Dave's phone call reporting on Buck's first pheasant hunt. He was full of his usual enthusiasm and described hunting pheasants over Buck as "a religious experience." I guess that's as close as you can come to extolling the virtues of a dog!

CHAPTER **6**

FORCE-FETCHING

NOW COMES THE TURNING POINT in your relationship with your dog. Up to now your dog has recognized you as a companion, thanks to walks and other activities, and has accepted your authority to a certain extent through the obedience commands. However cooperative they may be, retrievers at this stage still withhold a portion of their allegiance and cooperation. Often this shows up in an imperfect delivery. We can change this by force-fetching a dog;, that is, by converting retrieving from a game your puppy does when and how he pleases, to a job that he performs reliably and on your command. Despite the fact that the procedure takes the "play" out of retrieving, we find that, once it is finished, dogs appear to love retrieving more than ever.

The process of force-fetching brings about several changes. First and most obvious, it improves a dog's delivery of birds and dummies. It is a good preventative of mouth problems such as dropping or playing with birds, and gives you the means to resolve many other problems that may develop. Second, force-fetching is conditioning the dog to respond to "pressure" positively and confidently by driving hard for a dummy on the ground, and later, in the force-on-back procedure, by going when sent despite conditions that may be forbidding. As such, it provides the foundation for teaching blind retrieves. Third, it brings about an improvement in attitude, which seems almost like a "brain transplant" in some dogs. The requirement that a dog yield control over his mouth to the trainer is a greater and more intrusive demand than any you have made so far. It is natural for the dog to resist, and most dogs do. By the time the trainer has patiently overcome all of the dog's efforts to resist, the dog accepts the new level of control, and works with the trainer with a much greater degree of cooperation than before.

Making "Fetch" a command that your dog clearly understands also leads to greater confidence than is possible otherwise. When training becomes confusing or stressful (perhaps the dog is corrected for going to the wrong place, or for breaking), the dog's understanding of the fetch command provides a way out of the confusion, a resolution to the stress. The dog knows that completing the retrieve is the right thing to do. While the prospect of systematically applying pressure (pain) to a pet is unappealing to most owners, force-fetching is far more humane in the long run than is neglecting to do so. The unpleasantness, to a dog, of being confused, knowing something is expected but not knowing what, must not be underestimated. Most dogs seem much more distressed at this kind of confusion than they are by moderate pain applied in a straightforward manner. By force-fetching, and by fair, step-by-step training following force-fetching, you give your dog the power to avoid confusion and "turn off" pressure.

Situational reprimand for issues involving bird-handling, pickup, delivery, and/or steadiness is unfair to a dog who lacks the foundation to understand clearly what his trainer desires. In practice, such treatment often leads to long-term, intractable problems. Some dogs quit retrieving altogether when treated this way; others may just lack confidence. Our recommendation is, therefore, that you force-fetch your dog!

Our force-fetching procedure works on a wide variety of dogs, including the softest Chesapeakes. While Labs are thought to be "forgiving" dogs, and some may be successfully rushed through by increasing the pressure, we do not recommend this, particularly for novice trainers. Most trainers who force-fetch dogs very quickly are experienced in reading a dog's responses and knowing when enough is enough. Some dogs (including some Labs) simply cannot take this treatment. We feel, therefore, that if you are not experienced in this phase of training, you are wise to be conservative and progress slowly.

The first key to successful force-fetching is to judge progress by your dog's response at each step, not according to what you have done or a timetable of predicted results. Dogs vary widely in the time it takes to master force-fetch, and progress depends further on the trainer: how effectively he or she communicates with the dog, consistency of work, etc. Be sure your dog has fully mastered each step before attempting the next. Don't get hung up on trying to get the job done fast — focus instead on what a good, reliable retriever your dog is going to be.

The second key is patience. Most retrievers will try your patience! Progress in force-fetching is not steady, but tends to go in jumps and breakthroughs, with periods of no apparent progress in between. At some point, or at several points, the lack of correct response is likely to make you feel that you are in a struggle or contest with your dog, and by golly, you are going to win! But the way to win is through patience. With continual insistence, you will outlast all of your dog's explorations of how not to "fetch" properly. Do not be in a hurry. Skipping or short cutting steps will cost you much more time and frustration in the long run.

The third key is your dog's attitude. You can't put a good attitude in your dog later if you disregard it now. The only way to develop an eager, happy retriever is to maintain the dog's trust and enthusiasm throughout his training, including force-fetch. This is the most demanding phase of training the dog has yet faced. Your dog will find it stressful, but it doesn't have to be a miserable grind. Your goal is to teach a productive and confident response to training pressure. A good way to manage the stress level while keeping your dog focused on work is to review obedience exercises he knows and can do with confidence, earning your praise. Drills involving movement, such as heeling and coming when called, are particularly good for bringing a dog "up." Begin or end sessions with a "freebie" if you can get the dummy from your dog's mouth. If he spits the dummy out, better to suspend all retrieving until he will deliver to hand (usually soon after your work on *hold* is completed).

Of course, the most important strategy to keep your dog making progress and prevent his being overwhelmed is the very theme of this book: *keep sessions short*. The portion of a training session devoted to force-fetch should be no more than five minutes. Use an egg timer if necessary. Ensure that each session ends with success, even if this means simplifying your requirements (fewer distractions on *hold*; a shorter reach on *fetch*) or ending a session at three minutes if your dog has just done something especially well. You can continue with obedience review for the remainder of your ten minutes, or you may feel that it is better to put your dog up and give him a chance to think about what he has just done. As always, wild play sessions after training serve to undermine that training, and should be avoided. In this phase of training, consistency of work is especially important. Train at least once every day, and make an extra effort not to skip any sessions.

We recommend suspending field work during the time you are force-fetching your dog. If he has the opportunity to indulge bad habits such as dropping the dummy, force fetching will take longer and be more stressful for both of you.

Before beginning force-fetch, your dog's permanent teeth must be fully in so that he can hold a dummy firmly without pain. He must have mastered basic obedience: *heel, sit, stay,* and coming when called (*here*). Most important is his response to the "Sit" command. He must sit promptly and completely upon a single command, and remain sitting quietly at your side despite distractions.

It is easiest if your dog wears a choke or pinch collar, to which a check cord is attached, and a wide (1") buckle collar (the e-collar works well) adjusted to be snug and ride high on his neck behind his head.

Accepting the Dummy

The first step in the procedure is getting your dog to accept the dummy that you place in his mouth. This step may be anything from trivially easy to a prolonged ordeal. Sit your dog at heel. Attempt to place the dummy in your dog's mouth as follows: with your left hand on top of your dog's muzzle, find the indentation in the gum behind the upper canine teeth. With your right hand, place the dummy against the front of your dog's mouth. Pull upward with your left hand while pressing in and downward with the dummy against your dog's chin with your right. As your dog's mouth begins to open, roll the dummy in over the lower canine teeth. Say, "Hold" and cage his mouth with your right hand. Most dogs respond with some degree of head movement, open their mouths wide to drop the dummy,

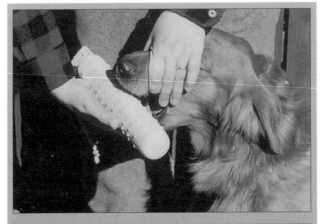

Gently open your dog's mouth. . .

. . . then roll in the dummy, hold his mouth closed, and praise.

try to push it away with their tongue, etc. If, in his efforts to resist, your dog stands up, forget the dummy and give an emphatic sit correction while saying, "Sit!" Then start over. If your dog repeatedly stands up to struggle, back up and work on obedience some more. You may find it helps to switch from a choke to a pinch collar.

As soon as your dog relaxes and accepts the situation, praise him, then take the dummy out of his mouth while saying, "Leave it!" Heel forward a few steps, sit your dog, and repeat.

As we have mentioned previously, an important principle of

*Make a loop
out of your dog's
check cord. . .*

*. . . and snug it
up to prevent
him from
spitting the
dummy out.*

training is to avoid getting into any protracted physical struggles with a dog. If your dog is committed to fighting introduction of the dummy into his mouth, put a loop of his check cord around his muzzle before putting in the dummy (see photo sequence). Pull to tighten the check cord, and your dog is now fighting the cord instead of you. While many dogs succeed in spitting the dummy out, repetition of this procedure usually gets them to accept the dummy satisfactorily, often in one session or sometimes requiring two or three days.

Holding the Dummy

Next, you need to get your dog not only to accept, but also to hold the dummy — firmly, without dropping it, first while sitting still and then while walking and running. This is a particularly frustrating step, not so much because dogs resist it as because communicating what you want seems inefficient and slow. Persist and be patient though. This is the most important part of force-fetching. When John started training years ago, this constituted the whole of the procedure. Continuing before a dog is solid on holding can lead to nervous snapping at the dummy or bird followed by spitting it out, or to incessant chomping and rolling, even crushing birds (hardmouth). Dogs vary tremendously in the time needed to learn a reliable hold — from one session to over a month.

Once your dog is accepting the dummy without a struggle, place the dummy in his mouth, say "Hold," and support his jaw with a hand under his chin to prevent his dropping the dummy. Praise your dog — tell him, "Good!" while rubbing his ears with the other hand. After about four or five seconds, take hold of the dummy with your right hand, say "Leave it!", and roll the dummy out of your dog's mouth (never snatch the dummy away). Heel your dog forward and repeat. Holds should start out fairly brief: ultimately you want to condition your dog to like having a dummy in his mouth, so don't prolong it to the point where it becomes distasteful.

Next you want to get your dog to take responsibility for holding the dummy. When your dog is comfortable with the five-second hold with your hand supporting his chin (often in the first session), lower your hand briefly and, if his hold slackens, quickly bring your hand back up to close his mouth and repeat "Hold!" If your dog lowers his head, raise it back up when you return your hand to his chin.

Keep your right hand ready to support your dog's chin or to correct, as needed.

As long as you support your dog's chin, you are taking responsibility for his holding the dummy. After a couple of sessions when your dog has had the opportunity to understand that you want the dummy to stay in his mouth, you can start using corrections to make him responsible for holding the dummy. Now when you place the dummy in your dog's mouth and lower your hand from his chin, allow your dog to drop the dummy and, as soon as the dummy leaves his mouth, chuck your dog under the chin with your ever-ready right hand while saying "No!" For a cooperative or young dog, use a fairly gentle tap — he will understand your disapproval. Quickly put the dummy back in your dog's mouth and repeat, "Hold."

Mix up holds with correction and holds where you "rescue" your dog from his mistake by supporting his chin. Most dogs act confused at first and may seem to conclude that having the

Using a training stick to increase a dog's concentration on holding the dummy.

dummy in their mouth is a bad thing. Using more help than correction seems to make this stage go more smoothly. If your dog progresses to quickly spitting out the dummy and ducking away, you are using too much correction and not enough help. Praise your dog when the dummy is in his mouth, whether the dog is holding on his own or whether you are supporting it. Continue to heel forward frequently after doing one to three holds in one spot. As your dog learns, lengthen the duration of holds, but continue to keep the sessions short.

Don't be surprised if, as you progress with this stage, you find your dog clamping his mouth shut so that you need to pry it open to put the dummy in. This is usually associated with a firmer grip when holding. Take it as a sign you are making headway.

As your dog gets the idea, increase his responsibility. Walk out front, then all the way around your dog as he sits holding the

Tap the end of the dummy to teach him to tighten his grip.

dummy. With a stick, tap and stroke your dog's body, neck, even legs. This helps teach your dog that he must concentrate on holding regardless of distractions. Next use the stick to tap the ends of the dummy. Your dog should respond by tightening his grip (praise him!). You can also jerk the dummy cord lightly while saying "Hold." Here is where you can make some headway with a slack-mouthed dog or one that rolls and chomps the dummy. Tap the dummy when it is dangling or when your dog is rolling it. If your dog drops it, chuck him solidly under the chin, say "No! Hold!" and put the dummy back in place.

Moving While Holding

Getting your dog to hold the dummy while moving is a challenge. If you tell your dog to "Heel" while he is holding the dummy, the likely response is to spit out the dummy and trot along beside you, tail high. He appears to be thinking, "Oh, what a relief. Back to plain old simple heeling and done with this stressful dummy-in-the-mouth stuff!" It works better to get your dog moving without a command. Help your dog by putting your right hand under his chin, pull forward on his lead with your left, and repeat, "Hold." Your dog will probably act confused, so make sure you support his jaw and praise him as soon as he begins to move. Don't go far — a couple of steps is plenty the first time. Have your dog sit and "Leave it."

Most dogs seem convinced that the "Hold" command entails sitting in one place. Usually they resist being pulled forward, and may shake their heads trying to get rid of the dummy. Keep working, holding your dog's mouth closed as you force him to move and praise him, until all signs of resistance or confusion subside. If your dog really fights to get rid of the dummy, hooking your finger in the angle of bone under his chin may help you keep his mouth properly closed. Once you start getting your dog moving while holding the dummy, do not do any heeling without the dummy. After you get your dog to go the required distance, have him sit, praise him, accept the dummy (as always, with a "Leave it" command), then let him sit by your side and rest for a few seconds before repeating.

The key to smooth progress at this point is to continue helping support the dummy in your dog's mouth until he is walking confidently while holding the dummy. Next, try holding your hand in front of your dog's muzzle as the two of you move. Most drops should be corrected merely with "No," replacing the dummy in your dog's mouth, and repeating "Hold" — with only an occasional chuck on the chin to remind your dog that you "mean it." Soon your dog will get the idea and you can take your hand away. Keep working until your dog can go over obstacles at a fast trot or lope without dropping the dummy. Have him come to heel position and

Support your dog's chin, pull on the lead to get him moving...

...and praise.

sit while holding. For all this movement, use body language rather than verbal commands ("sit" usually does not cause a problem).

While none of these steps should be skipped or shortcut, it sometimes works to get your dog moving with the dummy before using the stick to create distractions. This is especially good for dogs who quickly learn to hold the dummy tightly without chomping and rolling it. For dogs with more nervous mouths, work with them sitting until they will hold the dummy firmly and still.

The Fetch Command: Taking the Dummy

When your dog holds the dummy firmly without rolling or chomping it at a walk and at a run you are ready to introduce the fetch command. The introduction to fetch is not difficult, but it is important for what follows. As when you were beginning the hold, place the dummy in your dog's mouth, but this time say "Fetch!" as you do so. Give your dog a chance to get a good grip on the dummy and hold it for a second or two, then take the dummy as you say, "Leave it!". Continue to include movement and an occasional longer hold. Five to ten repetitions of "Fetch!" in one spot could be followed by holding while heeling to a new spot. Use your judgment regarding praise in this stage; for some dogs it is motivating, but others are distracted by it. You can always praise a dog that sits to deliver after an extended hold.

Devote enough repetitions so that you are sure your dog understands that "Fetch" means "the dummy goes in your mouth." Now get ready for a session that may require some time, and must be seen through. It is time to expand the meaning of "Fetch" to mean, "open your mouth and accept the dummy." Start with a review of the "Fetch"/"Leave it" routine. Then sit your dog, grasp hold of the tight buckle collar with your left hand, hold the dummy in front of his mouth with your right hand, and say, "Fetch" as you press the dummy against his lips. Most likely your dog will open his mouth and allow you to roll the dummy in. He may resist and clamp his mouth shut. This is fine, except that you are going to keep up the pressure until you overcome the resistance. Repeat the word, "Fetch" in a calm voice at intervals. When his clenched mouth slackens, quickly roll in the dummy.

Continue to practice until your dog readily opens his mouth on command. Now you are ready to progress to what most people think of as force-fetching: the ear pinch. You will use the ear pinch to make your dog reach forward to take the dummy.

Remember, though, that you are not just using pressure to get the desired response; you are teaching your dog to respond to pressure by making a retrieve. Some dogs, particularly many Labs, seem preprogrammed to respond to pressure constructively. With many others, however, it is important not just to assume the pressure will work, but to adjust the amount, timing, and duration so as to get the best response.

As always, begin your training session with some review. Then sit your dog. Take hold of his buckle collar and ear as follows. Slide the last three fingers of your left hand towards your dog's head under the collar, and curl them over the collar to grasp it firmly. With your thumb and index finger, pull your dog's left ear back over the collar (inside up) and hold it there gently. The "ear pinch" is administered by pressing with your thumbnail at the boundary between hair and bare skin (don't pinch yet). Depending on the size and strength of your hands, you may want to press against the collar or against your index finger.

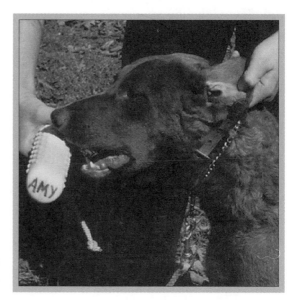

Administering the ear-pinch.

Hold the dummy in front of your dog's mouth. Say "Fetch" while pressing the dummy against his lips and pinching his ear. If your dog opens his mouth, roll the dummy in and quickly let off the ear pressure as you do. Praise him. You want him to get the idea that the ear-pinch means, "get that dummy in your mouth!"

We usually start with a light pinch — a little pressure with the thumbnail. Often there is no sign that the dog even feels the pinch. This is fine — the pinch will begin as a slight distraction as you ask your dog to repeat what you have already taught. As you start to pinch a little harder, it will become a bigger distraction and your dog may resist opening his mouth. Your goal is to make the pinch into an effective means of force. You can do this effectively by gradually increasing the pressure once the pattern of "fetch command—pinch—get the dummy" has been established. As you increase the pinching pressure, make sure your dog continues to respond by opening his mouth.

If your dog clenches his mouth shut, you have an opportunity to show him you are determined. Keep pinching and press the dummy harder against his lips. Repeat "Fetch." As always, keep your voice calm. Persist! Eventually your dog will give in and open his mouth. Be ready, roll that dummy in, stop the ear pressure, and praise him. Fortunately, you usually don't have to fight this battle more than once (perhaps because the ear is getting tender, or the dog has decided it isn't worth it). After a fetch command, your dog (not you) should be holding the dummy. Tell him to "Leave it" as you take it away.

Reaching Forward to Take the Dummy

If your dog puts up much resistance, just do 10 - 15 repetitions and end the session. Once he complies readily, then after a few repetitions, pinch his ear and say "Fetch" but hold the dummy still and maintain ear pressure. When your dog moves his head forward, even a tiny amount, reward him by placing the dummy in his mouth and release the pressure. Repeat a few times, delaying and decreasing your movement of the dummy toward your dog's mouth. With a few repetitions of this, most dogs will readily learn to reach forward a couple of inches and take the dummy — the new meaning of "Fetch." Try to avoid pushing your dog's head forward. You want the forward momentum to come from him. Soon he will try to grab the dummy before you can pinch him. Hold him back by the collar until you give the command. As when we restrain young dogs on marks, this restraint will increase his forward drive.

Start mixing in instances in which you give the command and stop holding your dog back, but do not pinch his ear. Try not to be predictable about when you do and do not pinch — maybe pinch twice in a row, then do three fetches with no pinch. You want your dog to think that he is "beating the pinch" by getting the dummy fast. Any time he is slow, pinch! Now you can use a new standard for knowing when it is time to progress: if your dog is reliable at one level after several repetitions without a pinch, he is probably ready to move on.

Start holding the dummy four or five inches in front of your dog when you say "Fetch." When he is solid reaching this far, hold the dummy farther forward. Soon he will have to stand up in order to reach far enough. When he must stand up, tell your dog to "Hold," then "Sit" with the dummy before telling him to "Leave it." If you hold him back by the collar before giving the "Fetch" command, he should start lunging aggressively for the dummy when the restraint is removed. If he doesn't, you may be trying to advance too fast — back up and work on a shorter reach. Be sure you are in position with your hold on the collar and ear every time you give the command, whether you plan to pinch or not.

Hold the dummy in front of your dog so he must lunge forward to grab it.

When your dog will lunge three feet and grab the dummy, whether you pinch his ear or not, you are ready to work towards picking the dummy up from the ground.

Picking the Dummy up from the Ground

This is another area where resistance is common. It seems that picking up an object from the ground requires a far greater subordination of will than does grabbing it from your hand, and most dogs need some convincing. We try to break it down into several parts: holding the dummy lower, holding just above the ground, holding by the string with one end on the ground, dummy on the ground with your hand touching one end, and finally dummy lying on the ground.

Progress through the different holding positions as before: when your dog is solid and reliable, move on to the next. If your

Keeping your hand on the dummy until just before your dog picks it up helps to ease the transition.

dog fetches well from the ground when your hand is on the dummy but refuses when it is not, you can break this step down farther by having your hand on the dummy when you give the "Fetch" command, then removing it just before the dog gets the dummy. Then progress to removing your hand sooner and sooner after the "Fetch" command, then just before the "Fetch" command, to the point where you can just toss the dummy down. Make sure that when the dummy starts contacting the ground, it does not get dirty or sandy. Dogs don't like the feeling of grit in their teeth. Working on a lawn will keep it clean.

Common Problems

As you make progress with the fetch command, getting your dog to reach farther and lower, he is likely to show some reaction to the pressure you are imposing. Instead of heeling perfectly at your side when your dog is carrying the dummy, he will probably forge ahead, straining at the leash. We feel it is best not to make an issue of heeling at this point. To do so would add more stress to the force-fetch procedure and might confuse your dog. Another common reaction is reluctance to sit between fetches. Since "Sit" needs to be extremely reliable in a working retriever, we do enforce it, but we suggest making it easier on your dog by not requiring a sit after every fetch, but perhaps after one in five or so. You may also find that when you throw a "freebie," your dog runs out to it but does not pick it up. If you turn your back and pretend to ignore both dog and dummy, he may feel enough at ease to retrieve it. Turn around as you hear him returning, praise him, and you may find that he delivers to hand.

If your dog is one that totally balks at picking the dummy up off the ground, and you have tried going back to review previous steps, you might make some headway by giving in a little. Toss a dummy forward enough to be a short freebie and release your dog. Repeat, but say "Fetch" as you release him. Repeat, shortening the distance — approaching the problem from the opposite direction, as it were. Sometimes simply kicking the dummy to move it forward a little is all that is needed. Intuitively it seems as though your dog must be forced through every part of this procedure, but experience shows that relenting a little at this point may be just as effective.

Some dogs will not respond to "easing up" with a short throw, but will squeal, thrash around, and direct their efforts to escaping the ear pinch by every possible means except getting the dummy. Some hook their paws over the trainer's forearm in an attempt to prevent the trainer from pinching the ear. Some leap up and snap in the air alarmingly close to the trainer's hands and face. The more this kind of behavior is allowed to continue, the more your dog will become convinced that it is a viable means of resisting your demands. As mentioned previously, it is important not to establish a pattern of struggling with your dog physically.

The most effective way to deal with this kind of resistance is to temporarily simplify your demands while enforcing them convincingly. If the trouble comes when the dummy is on the ground, go back to a three-foot reach at the dog's level. Stand with your foot on the check cord so your dog cannot rear up. Pinch hard every time — use the highest level of pressure you have previously found to be effective. Do this for several sessions, then ease back into a pattern of pinching some of the time, and letting your dog succeed without a pinch some of the time.

If your dog continues to struggle with you instead of reaching for the dummy, you will have to restrain him effectively. One way to do this is to attach a bolt snap to a stationary object such as a fence post or a cable strung between two trees. Clip the snap to your dog's choke collar and he will be able to move only a few inches. Continue to keep the sessions short. The object here is to establish the habit of responding to pressure by driving for the dummy, and to eliminate other responses.

Reinforcement with the E-Collar in Force Fetching

An alternative way of dealing with the dog who struggles is to go to the e-collar in place of the ear pinch. One advantage of using the e-collar is that your dog cannot anticipate the shock and react apprehensively, as he may when you take hold of his ear. Another advantage is that there is no obvious way to fight the shock, and most dogs do not try, especially when the collar is properly introduced. Ordinarily, we hold off on e-collar use until force-fetching is complete, but it can be an excellent solution for these "fighters."

Devote a couple of sessions to reviewing the beginnings of the fetch command, where the dummy is held right in front of your dog's mouth. After a couple of repetitions of "Fetch" at this distance, add a brief continuous nick with the "low" button, immediately following the "Fetch" command. Once you get your dog responding to the "Fetch"/nick by grabbing the dummy, keep practicing and extending the distance. Limit sessions to 10 - 15 nicks with the collar. Experiment a little — some dogs respond better if the nick slightly precedes the "Fetch" command, while others respond best when it follows the command. Allow at least three sessions to build the right response before working up to the level where the resistance occurred.

If you so choose, you can finish force-fetch using the e-collar instead of the ear pinch. Do not, however, address refusals by escalating the intensity and duration of shock. Better to lower your expectations a step or two and progress more slowly, making sure you are getting the desired response to the shock at each step.

By the time the issue of picking up from the ground is resolved, most dogs will dive on the dummy when you say "Fetch," but many will fumble it, lie down, or just be very slow to come up with it. This is continued resistance to your increasing authority, and the job is not done until it is overcome. As your dog lunges forward toward the dummy, move forward yourself so he remains in the heel position. As soon as his jaws reach the dummy, pull his head up with your hand on the collar. This works best if you continue moving forward a step or two past where the dummy was lying. If your dog drops the dummy, correct — use a chuck under the chin or pinch his ear and place the dummy in his mouth. If he doesn't make rapid progress, you can increase the pressure by requiring him to pick up the dropped dummy (stay on his ear until he does).

Some dogs progress smoothly throughout force-fetching. They never seem to put up the resistance described in the previous few paragraphs, but just seem to learn, cooperate, and progress readily from step to step. Dogs who resist mightily and then give in are often the most reliable and the quickest to advance after forcing. With the "easy" dogs, it is hard to tell whether the lesson has been learned or the dog has just been "going through the motions." The next step, "Stick-fetch," differentiates these two possibilities, identifying the sandbaggers and giving the trainer an opportunity to correct. Most dogs refuse the fetch command at the beginning of the stick-fetch procedure, but some of the easy dogs then continue to refuse the command under simpler circumstances. If your dog is one of these, back up as far as you need to, and continue with as much pressure as is needed to overcome the resistance which has finally surfaced. You might try using the e-collar instead of the ear pinch the second time around.

Stick-Fetch

Stick-fetch accomplishes two things: it teaches your dog that distractions are no excuse to ignore a fetch command, and it transfers much of the momentum-producing power of the ear pinch to the stick, thus providing a basis for force-on-back.

Use a regular training stick for this step. You can have a helper wield the stick or do it yourself. Don't make the stick any more obvious than it has to be — the point is not to threaten your dog. With your dog at heel, toss the dummy about three feet in front of your dog. With your hand on the collar and ear, say "Fetch." Immediately tap your dog on the hindquarters with the stick. Repeat "Fetch" and pinch his ear all the way to the dummy. Repeat, varying whether or not you hit your dog. Again, you want to make your dog think that by going fast he can avoid the stick. As he catches on, try using the stick and no ear pinch. Usually, not many sessions are needed (maybe 3 - 6). When your

The "stick-fetch."

dog is digging out to beat the stick and seems totally reliable without any ear pinch, you are finished.

If you are training with the e-collar but have not resorted to using it before now, we recommend that you go back to the shortest possible "Fetch" and do a brief review of force-fetching, using the e-collar for enforcement. Use the procedure described above and allow three or four training days with not more than fifteen nicks per session for this "recap." Be careful not to overdo the "collar-force-fetch." Occasionally we see dogs in trials who "freeze" on birds, refusing to give them up. While we have never had this problem in a dog we force-fetched, it is widely believed to be the result of too much pressure in this stage of training, and we see no reason to dispute that. Once a dog is forced, he is forced, and pouring on extra pressure does nothing to improve the situation.

Walking Fetch

We recommend following force-fetch with a walking fetch drill where several dummies are lying on the ground, ten feet or more apart. Approach the dummies with your dog at heel and say, "Fetch" as his attention focuses on the first dummy. Correct any refusals with the ear pinch (or e-collar). After your dog sits to deliver, you can drop the dummy behind him for a later circuit. When his performance is smooth, the stick can be added just as in the fetch from a sitting position. If the previous steps have been carefully done, your dog will soon be lunging eagerly for each dummy as soon as he sees it.

Next work on getting your dog to wait until he is commanded to "Fetch," using repeated "Heel" commands and jerks on the lead. Do not begin to do this, though, until your dog is showing a lot of anticipation — towing you to the next dummy in the sequence as soon as the present dummy is out of his mouth. Generally we don't pursue "waiting for the command" to perfection. We have just put a lot of work, and pressure on the dog, into making him anxious to grab dummies. We don't want to undermine this idea — better to let it become habit first.

The "walking fetch" drill makes the transition to picking up a dummy your dog finds on the ground, not only one that has just been thrown. Now he can be sent to a pile, the foundation for forcing-on-back and for blind retrieves. His experience with the stick and e-collar have prepared him to respond to forcing on back with either of these tools. He can be sent, with appropriate hand signals, to side and back piles, making an introduction to casting. And, of course, your dog should deliver perfectly and you, as trainer, have the tools to enforce this: command "Hold" as he emerges from water and considers putting the bird down to shake, and insist that he "Fetch" if a dummy or bird is ever dropped.

FORCE-FETCHING

by John

SOME DOGS SEEM ALMOST IMPOSSIBLE TO FORCE FETCH. I use the word "seem" advisedly. In actual practice, almost any dog can be force fetched. The fact that the process in some extremely difficult cases may take months does not mean that they can't, or won't, get it right — in time. Tarheel Jade was one of the many examples of an individual who did not, despite high intelligence, seem to be able to put two and two together on the force fetch program. I tried for many weeks to get Jade to hold the dummy, without success. The instant my hand came away from her chin where I was supporting the dummy in her mouth, she would spit it out.

In frustration, I moved from trying to get her to hold the dummy to forcing her to take it out of my hand on command. I bore down on her with the ear pinch, to which she showed little response, and once more, failed to make any headway. After pursuing every avenue of force fetching I could think of, one afternoon I threw up my hands on the whole project and left the house in a state of disgust. I had done all of my force fetching efforts with Jade in the living room.

I was gone for several hours and when I returned home my wife announced that Jade was now force fetched (or force broke, as we used to call it). I was doubtful, but when she placed a dummy on the floor and told Jade, "Fetch it," Jade dove on the dummy, picked it up, and held it perfectly. I have never been able to understand how Jade learned this in one afternoon after showing no progress for weeks — but there it was. Seeing is believing.

Other dogs show a steady, if extremely slow, progress on forcing. We had a Viszla in training about eight years ago who had everything she needed to complete her FC except placements in the event in which retrieving of the flushed and shot bird is required. This dog had absolutely no interest in chasing, catching, or retrieving anything, so force fetching her was a challenging project. My son, Anton, worked with her every day for about four months, and although she showed weekly progress, it was so gradual that you had to wonder if it would ever get done.

We progressed from the forcing table with a wooden dowel as the retrieving object, to a cloth dummy, then a plastic dummy, and finally a plastic dummy with duck or pheasant wings attached with strapping tape. Each change of retrieving objects seemed to set her back to square one and the work of ear pinch and fetching started all over.

When we reached the stage of using dead birds with this Viszla she rebelled once again and by then, we were reaching the end of our expectations for success as well as those of the owner. Perseverance paid off, however, and we saw her through to live shot birds, both pheasants and chukars, including cripples.

This dog's love of chasing game came to life toward the end of her work with birds at which time she magically made a transformation from, "What, me pick up that thing?" to "Let me at 'em." Her work became so proficient on retrieving game that she quickly made her field championship on the weight of her retrieving expertise on some especially difficult birds.

A few dogs, very few in fact, seem to accept the force fetching training with such rapidity it seems that you haven't done any real training. Some of these dogs seem to be born to grab whatever you put in front of them, and hold it until you take it from them. Sunny (Mountain Run Rise 'N Shine MH) was one of these. His force fetching went so fast that I have trouble remembering any of it. I think it took two short afternoon sessions of saying "Fetch it," and "Hold it." Sunny's brief training on this phase of work held up when he was forced on back, which was surprising because usually it requires some pressure on force fetch to establish a basis of force for the force-on-back procedure. Sunny had a natural mouth, which I don't think is bred for as carefully as it should be in most present-day retrievers. When he was only three months of age he would carry a full-grown mallard around as long as I would allow it, and never chew or mishandle it.

Dummies could never escape Sunny's attention. If there was one anywhere in the training yard, he would find it and come running with it. Sunny was an embarrassment at field trials because if you turned him loose to air where the vehicles were parked, he would be back in a flash with a dummy out of someone else's van.

There was a time when we worried more about too aggressive (hard) a mouth than we did about forcing retrievers to pick things up. I recall reading in some of the old dog training books on the subject of force breaking, and scratching my head in wonderment as to why you would need to force a dog to do something it wanted to do in the first place. We sought after dogs with a "soft" mouth—those we could get the bird away from in one piece, and considered it a triumph if a duck was brought to hand not punched full of teeth holes. I had Chesapeakes at the time that could devour a small bird like a pigeon before you could get to them to make a correction. Some Labs were that way, too, but few goldens.

One of the worst of these was Sheba, a keen little Chesapeake bitch who was doing a great job on puppy retrieves with dummies. She showed no sign of a rough mouth until birds came into the picture. Her first retrieve on a dead bird was thrown in my back yard at a distance of about 20 feet. Sheba ran to the bird and started eating it. By the time I reached her, the last tip of a wing feather was disappearing down her throat. It made no difference what I tried with Sheba. I could have her at heel, offer her a bird, and before I could react to take it from her, she would have it half swallowed. I never solved the mouth problem with Sheba, and finally gave her away as a pet.

Today we see many loose-mouthed dogs who can't seem to hold a dummy or bird for more than a few steps. In cases like these, a 100-yard retrieve may consist of ten to fifteen pick-ups and drops on the way back to the handler. Woody (Oak Hill Deerwood), a golden retriever, was one of these when he was young. Most of the dogs we have had that possessed this "dropsy" problem grew out of it after they were force-fetched and had achieved a couple of years of age. This was the case with Woody. He now has an excellent mouth, only occasionally bobbling a dummy on delivery.

Once in a while you will see a retriever that seems to have no interest in retrieving whatsoever, but who comes to life after the force fetch program is applied. Guinness, a golden bitch, fit this description. We got Guinness in training from a client in Virginia who wanted a gun dog. She showed no signs of interest in dummies or birds, so we embarked first on an obedience program followed by a course of force-fetching.

Her first response to the leash and to training was to roll over on her back and go motionless. The solution we found was to pick her up bodily and place her in a sitting position while giving the command, "Sit." This procedure worked and when she reached a point where she would sit quickly on command with no tendency to roll over, we introduced the "Hold" command with the dummy in her mouth. Guinness learned this fairly quickly so we followed with the "Fetch" command using the e-collar for pressure because the ear-pinch failed to yield a result.

Guinness was quick to learn. As soon as it was established with her that "Sit" meant sit, and "Fetch" meant fetch, she quickly became an avid retriever. In about four months we were able to send her home accompanied by a video of her doing double marked retrieves on land and water with ducks and pigeons. She could also line and handle a little at that time. I'm sure that Guinness made a fine little gun dog. I am equally sure that if it were not for force fetching, she never would have retrieved at all.

CHAPTER

7

REFINEMENT
IN THE FIELD

WITH THE BIG STEP OF FORCE-FETCHING now complete, there still remain several subjects your retriever must master in order to operate smoothly in the field. These include steadiness, going straight (honesty), and going reliably when sent. In this chapter, we outline procedures for teaching and enforcing these important concepts, as well as easy introductions to details such as boats, decoys, and duck calls.

If you suspended field work while force-fetching, now is the time to get your dog back in the field and work on marking concurrently with these topics. Do, however, take pains to be consistent: do not let your retriever break (depart before she is sent) on marks, and continue to avoid temptations to cheat water or cover until you have prepared her for enforcement of the correct line. Progress continues to be dependent upon steady work. We recommend daily sessions, as always no more than ten minutes, on the material in this chapter. Where the suggested procedures do not involve marks, by all means set up separate sessions to practice marking as helpers are available. Suggestions for marking practice may be found in Chapter 8.

Steadying

We recommend beginning with steadying for the practical reason that a steady dog is much easier to work with in subsequent training. Steadiness simply means that your dog sits still until ordered to retrieve, resisting any impulse to break for a fallen bird or dummy. Steadying may begin as soon as force-fetching is complete; once you have the means to tell the dog to "go," you can begin teaching her to "wait."

Why steady a dog? There are multiple reasons a retriever should sit still until sent for a bird, of which safety is the foremost. A dog that is leaping uncontrollably about the blind or boat and getting out in front of the shooters prematurely is apt to cause a dangerous situation for himself and the hunters. Rocking boats, spilled coffee, guns knocked over, hunters thrown off balance, or a dog leaping into the air after a flushed pheasant as someone draws down on it are all invitations to disaster.

Steadiness also improves marking, and, obviously, control when sending on a blind. Dogs who creep, jump around, or are otherwise unruly are generally sloppy markers, with few exceptions. Although the dog believes she has a mark, having seen the beginning trajectory of the bird's fall, if she does not sit and watch the bird to the ground she will not really know where she is going, and is apt to hunt sloppily or need help. Advanced training is difficult with unsteady dogs, as dogs in motion are essentially impossible to line up for a blind retrieve. Additionally, if you want to impress your hunting friends favorably, have a dog that is rock steady, but goes like a shot when sent. It looks good!

Before you begin teaching steadiness, your dog should be sitting and staying on command in the absence of serious temptation to move, such as a thrown bird. Your dog will also be coming reliably, of course, and will have been force-fetched. Prior to now, you will have been restraining her with the collar/seat-of-the-pants hold, or possibly with a check cord or slip cord. The slip cord can be re-implemented at any time during your dog's life as a brush-up for steadiness and line manners.

Do not expect to achieve real or permanent steadiness quickly. A few dogs can learn this quickly, but most need time to make it a habit. We hope, of course, your dog is not an unmotivated slow-poke who would just as soon sit as retrieve. Steadiness, like force-fetching, may require weeks of daily practice to achieve a satisfactory result. Don't believe that because your dog "acts" steady for a few days consecutively that the job is done. If you cease to pay attention to the problem before steadiness is fully ingrained, your dog will most likely revert to her former undisciplined behavior — and quickly.

Tools for teaching steadiness: training stick and short check cord.

Slip cord: fasten one end to your wrist, pass it through your dog's collar, and hold the free end.

The training stick is an excellent device for reinforcing steadiness, and it must be applied fairly liberally, if not harshly. Repeat "Sit," smack on the rump, "Sit" before the mark. After the mark is down, repeat "Sit"/smack/"Sit," put your hand down slowly beside the dog's head, and send her on her name or the "Back" command, whichever is your preference. This should be the first phase of real steadying and should be practiced with the aid of a slip cord or short check cord (which you can stand on) should you have to resort to physical restraint.

When you begin steadying and no longer need one or both hands to restrain your dog on marks, it is time to start using a hand gesture on the send. The purpose of the hand is often misunderstood. When a dog is looking in the right direction, on a

Hand position for sending a dog.

mark or blind, the handler puts his hand out above or beside the dog's head, confirming the direction and signaling that the send command is imminent. During steadying, you will work to convince your dog that she must only go when both the hand and verbal signals are given, by tempting her with one and not the other. Later the hand will always be followed by "Back," and you will establish a consistent rhythm, giving the "Back" command perhaps one or one-and-a-half seconds after placing your hand by your dog's head.

When you send your dog, your hand should move very little, if at all. You are not trying to propel your dog forward. Thanks to your careful preparation in building desire, forcing on back, and maintaining clarity of communication, she is primed to charge forward on command. The presence of your hand, followed by the "back" command, are sufficient. Excess movement will merely distract your dog. Refrain from trying to use your hand to adjust the direction of your dog's attention. Don't put your hand out until she is looking toward the right spot. The ability to confirm a direction, which you will develop using this procedure, will enable you to give your dog valuable assistance on memory birds, as well as effective lining on blind retrieves.

Throughout these early steadying lessons, it is wise to use a helper to throw birds and shoot the blank pistol. Dummies are okay, but a dog steadied only on dummies will be likely to break under the greater excitement of birds. Tar of Moon Lake used to break only on cock pheasants, a particularly exciting bird. This

Leave only a foot or two of slack in the long check cord — enough to give the dog a jolt, but not to injure her.

After your dog has sat still for one to several seconds, unclip the cord and send her. If she breaks on the hand signal with no command, the cord will bring her up short.

problem was solved by buying a couple dozen cock pheasants and practicing on those solely until Tar was steady.

We like the check cord tied to some stationary object, such as a tree or truck bumper, for the next phase of steadying. Allow only a foot or two of slack in the cord so there is no risk of injuring your dog. Give the sit command once before the mark is thrown and then say nothing more, letting the cord jolt her to a sudden stop if she tries to go. This procedure introduces a new rule: only if your dog sits still is she allowed to make the retrieve. The desired behavior is positively reinforced, and learning is usually rapid — but since you are attempting to change an established habit, backsliding is likely if you are inconsistent and allow (reward) any breaks.

With dogs who have had the preliminary work with the stick and the slip cord properly done, this phase may seem too easily learned, so you must introduce some extraordinary temptations to accomplish your end, which is to induce the dog to break against the cord. A close shot bird, say 10 to 15 yards, will get most of them going without being sent. Swinging your hand past the dog's head without a verbal command will sometimes cause a break. Each time you can get your dog to break, do nothing but calmly return her to the sit position by your side, have the bird picked up, and repeat. Dogs will often break when they hear the clip on the check cord snap shut as you remove it. Eliminate this as a cue by letting the clip close with a snap, but leave it attached to your dog's collar. Then, when you put your hand beside her head in preparation for the send, she will probably go before the verbal command is given. Repeat until she is never quite sure if she is hooked up or not, and be slow and methodical with your hand, making her wait a few seconds before she is sent. Most

Creeping: the dog has moved out in front of the handler. This can be a difficult problem if a dog is allowed to develop the habit — so don't let her.

Round out steadying with plenty of work on live birds.

dogs take only a few days to master this level of steadiness, at which time you are ready to introduce remote methods of reinforcement.

The electric collar is the most obvious tool of choice at this point, but we like to use a slingshot or a BB gun as a preliminary to the collar to make absolutely sure the dog understands the command and is on her way to forming permanent habits. A marble works well in the slingshot, or a pellet from a BB gun will make the point without penetrating your dog's hide.

Have a helper who is skilled in the use of a slingshot or BB gun stand inconspicuously behind you while you handle your dog. Your helper should shoot your dog in the rump immediately if she moves a muscle before you have placed your hand beside her head and given the back command. Also, if your dog starts to break, give the sit command again, have your helper hit her with the BB or marble, and immediately repeat the sit command: the "Sit"/smack/"Sit" pattern once again. This is an example of indirect pressure; your dog is corrected, while sitting properly, for the preceding misbehavior. Repeat this procedure a sufficient number of times until you are quite sure you can walk into the field and shoot a bird over your dog's head and she will remain motionless until sent.

If you are using the electric collar and your dog has been conditioned to collar correction, you can make use of the collar for occasional lapses in steadiness. The procedure is the same as it was throughout your earlier steadiness training, only "Sit"/nick/"Sit" replaces "Sit"/smack/"Sit." It may be unwise to shock your dog while she is in the act of breaking, or it may work well to burn her while she is on the move and call her back without completing the retrieve. This is a matter for experimentation, since dogs vary in their responses. In general, however, shocking a dog while she is moving, running, swimming, etc., is generally more confusing than getting her stopped, under control, and then administering indirect pressure. If you use the e-collar, do all of your training with the collar on the dog. Many individuals will require only occasional e-collar reinforcement, but they learn that it's there and they form good habits.

If you are training without the collar, simply continue to work on the positive-reinforcement principle: your dog gets to make the retrieve only if she is properly steady. In practice, this means finding a way to stop her once she has broken, or having your thrower run over and pick the bird up before she can get to it.

From here on your dog should be steady in training, hunting, and competitive events, with only an occasional need for remedial measures. Remember that if you are hunting with a partner and another dog, or are running field trials or hunt tests, your dog will be required to *honor* — to sit still while another dog makes a retrieve — so you must practice that as well. Usually, the admonition "No bird" is used to precede a situation in which a dog is required to be steady while another dog retrieves.

Preparation for Hunting: Boats, Decoys, and Calls

Some areas of work for the hunting retriever require simple familiarity with the conditions. This type of training is designed to prepare your dog in advance for things that are awkward, confusing, or difficult upon the first exposure. Blinds, boats and decoys all fall into this category. If you hunt your dog in a variety of situations it is a good idea to practice all of them so that your initial hunts will be easier for her.

Teach your dog to sit and stay, briefly, outside of the blind after she has delivered her bird, then give the release command, "Hie-on" or whatever, and she will shake off the excess mud and water outside rather than all over you and your equipment.

In the case of hunting from a boat, you will have to put up with some water shaken off in the boat, but you can minimize it by having your dog sit and stay in the far end of the boat while you return to the other end, then give the "Shake" command. Soon your dog will learn to stand up and shake while away from you. Remember, "Sit," or "Sit; Stay" must mean don't shake, don't move, until you give a release command. Most dogs, if hunted enough, will get into the habit of doing this dependably without further training.

Getting in and out of the boat is usually learned in one or two

This Chesapeake waits in the stern for her cue to shake.

Helping a dog into a boat.

lessons. To be sent from the boat simply requires doing it a few times until your dog realizes that it is no different than a water entry from any other place. The exception to this is hunting in big, wavy, cold, open water such as hunting sea ducks (scoters) in midwinter. There is something very forbidding about an endless vista of rough, cold water with no land in sight. No matter what kind of power-house water dog you think you have, be prepared for a "no-go" when you send her over the side after that 75-yard duck through a hundred decoys. If you plan to do this type of hunting, take the boat out in the summer on a rough day and get your dog used to it.

Getting in the boat from deep water requires a little practice but is easily taught. You simply get hold of your dog's collar and give her enough of a lift to get her forepaws over the gunwale of the boat. When your dog has a grip on the boat with her paws, bear down on the top of her head with one hand and the added forward weight will propel her smoothly into the boat. Then say, "Sit; Stay," return to your end of the boat, tell your dog to "Shake," and it's done. We like to receive the bird while the dog is still swimming as it avoids the possibility of her biting down with undue pressure while being hoisted into the boat.

Decoys can be very confusing to your dog if she does not have some form of advance preparation. Some dogs, of course, focus on the destination and seem impervious to distraction from blocks, anchor lines, wind socks, etc. Many more dogs handle them with aplomb only after becoming familiar with them in a controlled situation. Fortunately, educating a dog about decoys is usually straightforward.

We would not rely on the things they do at field trials or hunt tests as a model for preparation for shooting over decoys. Field trial judges in particular usually throw out one or two decoys in some obscure corner in order to comply with the rule book. The hunt tests we have attended have been somewhat less guilty of this shortcoming.

A sensible preliminary to working a dog through decoys is to spread a few out on the grass and walk your dog among them on lead with a training stick in hand. When she offers to so much as sniff a decoy, bat her on the nose lightly, saying "No, leave it." Then throw some bumpers or dead birds among the decoys for her to retrieve. Follow this up with a few obvious marks past a few decoys in the water. If your dog hangs up in the decoys, do

You can teach your dog to ignore the decoys and look for the dummy or bird on land first.

Then try an obvious setup in the water.

not reprimand her, just re-throw the mark until she gets the picture. After this preliminary exposure to decoys she will pay little attention to them. We have had some individuals at training clinics who have shown an uncontrollable desire to go after decoys, biting at them and punching them full of holes. This is aggravating and expensive, and can usually be prevented by a little advance work. Most dogs exhibit an uncanny ability to distinguish between a decoy, no matter how realistic, and a bird or retrieving dummy.

If you are sure you are going to shoot over a dozen or so

If you plan to hunt over a big spread of decoys, practice retrieves among, and beyond, a large flock.

decoys, you will need to train your dog through only a few decoys, but if you will be shooting over a big spread, you'd better have a good-sized flock out there — 50 or more. Setting up like this is time-consuming, but it will pay off on the opening day with a professional piece of work from your dog. Other types of decoys, wind sock geese, and field decoys of various types should be introduced according to the likelihood of your hunting under those conditions. Because a dog's natural tendency to interpret a change in conditions as a boundary she must not cross, practice retrieves through the entire spread and into the open water beyond.

Duck calls are another accouterment of hunting which are easily introduced. Blowing a call once or twice in training while requiring your dog to sit should suffice to prevent a startled reaction that might flare incoming birds. If you plan to run retriever hunt tests in which duck calls are used to herald a throw, usually from a hidden position, it is worthwhile to practice that in a few of your training sessions. Once your dog has learned to look in the direction of the call in anticipation of a mark, however, you do not need to continually practice with duck calls. It is preferable to work with a shot alone most of the time, maintaining the skill of locating the mark by the sound of the shot.

One may argue that blowing the duck call alerts the dog to incoming birds. Generally, a good dog learns to detect arriving waterfowl before the hunter does, being blessed with acute hearing and excellent vision.

Honesty: Going Straight to Marks

At this stage, it is necessary to pay some attention to honesty (going straight to the mark without running around water or other obstacles). Almost all retrievers are inclined to cheat. A Derby dog we trained recently was such a cheater that he saw all water as an opportunity to run around the shore, going and coming. We gave him some simplified training in honesty, with no hand signals, and in a short time he became one of the most honest dogs we have worked with.

The most significant refinements in this area will be made when your dog has been taught to take hand signals, but you can make good progress with honesty before reaching this level of sophistication. It will be easiest if you have been following the advice in Chapter 3 to avoid exposing your dog to temptation that can develop the cheating habit. If you have been following that advice, however, you are probably wondering when and how you and your dog can move beyond such limited retrieving setups. Now is the time, and the procedure is straightforward.

The system consists very simply of giving the "Sit" command with the whistle, then calling the dog in and repeating the mark. If your dog does not yet reliably sit on the whistle, practice that skill, using the stick or e-collar in a "tweet"/smack/"tweet" or "tweet"/nick/"tweet" pattern until it is reliable. Stopping the dog with a whistle prior to calling her in works much better than just calling her, trying to reverse her direction while she is running at full speed. Our Derby dog, Bart, had an immense amount of drive, and when he found he couldn't make the retrieve by running the shore, he quickly learned to take an honest line to his marks. He soon became exceptionally direct, going and coming. Less ambitious dogs may take longer to learn this lesson, but if they find, repeatedly, that attempting to go around is unproductive, they will give it up.

Various methods of teaching honesty other than the use of advanced handling techniques can be effectively employed. A helper stationed on the shore with a short cane pole can be used to ward the dog off on the return. This is done by splashing the water with the cane pole to push the dog back "out to sea," or by gently poking her in the side to accomplish the same end. Care must be used not to spook your dog off the helper, as a thrower in the field will be essential in teaching marking. Do it gently and use only as much correction as is necessary. It is better to back off rather than to set your dog back by pursuing a losing game.

Many youngsters are honest going out, but always swim to the far shore after picking up the dummy or bird, and run the shore back. Even though the dog has already picked up her mark, "cheating the return" is undesirable. On a multiple mark, a dog who cheats the return is apt to be confused about where she has been, plus shirking the water leads to a greater tendency to cheat going to marks. For these youngsters, we use a salt-water trolling reel and some heavy monofilament line on a short trolling rod. We feed line to the dog while she is going out, on free spool, and engage the return keeping the line taut enough on the return so that she cannot swim to the far shore and run the bank back.

This usually works after a few applications, but you must be careful not to haul on your dog too hard or you will pull her under, causing panic and undoing whatever good you may have accomplished. Just don't let your dog swim to the far shore. Guide her straight back.

Forcing on Back

Forcing on back is the last of the formal procedures needed to make a reliable retriever. It is often said that force fetching converts retrieving from a matter of play to a matter of obedience, but that is only partially true. Force fetching has mainly to do with a dog's mouth: the pickup, delivery, and bird-handling aspects of the retrieve. Going reliably when sent is a separate issue, and most dogs, even after force fetching, will refuse to go under some circumstances (usually a long retrieve, a confusing picture, or forbidding terrain). Forcing on back is an advanced parallel of force-fetching; it teaches that "going when sent" is not optional, but mandatory.

While forcing a dog on back is an advanced procedure — and one that carries a high risk of being done incorrectly — we start dogs on this at a fairly young age. The sooner a dog understands the command "Back" to be not merely permission to go get a bird or dummy, but a command that she must promptly and unfailingly obey, the sooner she will establish the right habits with the confidence of knowing what is expected of her. There is nothing more disconcerting than to give a dog the command to retrieve and have her sit there motionless — the "no-go." Experienced trainers despise this more than any other infraction. Once "Back" is understood as a command, many otherwise confusing situations may be resolved by commanding the dog to make the retrieve.

Force fetching, which we discussed in Chapter 6, is the basis for forcing on back and is necessary to any implementation of this command. First, simply extend the distance of the fetch command. We usually do an extended version of the stick fetch, sending the dog to a pile of dummies, progressing up to distances of 75 yards on our yard pattern. We show the pile to the dog and then back up gradually to the maximum distance. It is important to use the stick as enforcement at this stage. Restrain the dog with a short check cord and smack her on the rump two or three times sharply while repeating the command, "Back!" with each strike of the stick; then release her on the command "Back" and let her get the dummy. Most dogs will thrash to get away when this method is applied and will need remedial work on steadying after the program is completed.

Six dummies per session at 75 yards on land, or the distance of a long hand throw in the water, is about right for most dogs. Longer swims should be accompanied by a reduction in repetitions, perhaps only two retrieves at 100 yards, for example. Some dogs never respond to pressure very well, no matter how carefully you have force fetched. These dogs may require less of everything during forcing on back: fewer trips to the pile, slower progress from the pile back to your intended sending point 75 yards away, and less pressure. In extreme cases, two forced retrieves to the pile might each be followed with "marked" hand throws to the pile, following which the dog is put up. This kind of problem is most common in Chesapeake and golden bitches, but can occur in male or female of any breed. If you have problems with the fifth dummy picked up, stick to four for a few days.

You will know that you have forced on back adequately when you return to the field and find that your dog always goes on command, land or water. Most dogs will give a "no-go" somewhere along the way. At that point, you can administer the smack-smack with the "Back, back" in the field to reduce these occurrences. If it happens frequently, you are generally better off to return to the yard and add a week or so of extra work under rigidly controlled conditions until success is achieved. Most dogs with a lot of drive respond favorably to this form of training. They seem to take the attitude that they are being forced to do what they wanted to do in the first place.

We generally recommend e-collar reinforcement behind the sending line when forcing on back. Back up a few steps in the event of a no-go, then advance to the sending line while repeating the command "Heel." Nick your dog with the collar with each repetition of "Heel." Restrain her while repeating "Back"/nick/"Back" on the line a couple of times. This replaces the smack of the stick with the nick of the collar and will effectively condition her to a light shock in connection with the "Back" command.

It has been suggested that forcing on back is a matter of teaching the dog that nothing that happens as a result of going on a retrieve will be as bad as the consequences of not going. While we think of forcing on back more in terms of conditioning dogs to the habit of always going when sent, it is worth planning training sessions so that your dog is not subjected to a lot of punishment in the field, particularly at this stage of her training. As we suggested in the discussion of honesty, stopping your dog with the whistle and calling her back is often sufficient to put an end to an infraction, without resorting to physical pressure. Refrain from sending your dog through briars or into frigid water while forcing on back. It is neither necessary nor constructive to force her into forbidding conditions until later in her training, if at all.

Some trainers employ shock stimulation while the dog is on her way to the objective. This works well in some cases, but can affect some dogs' attitudes. We have had occasion, especially with extremely fast, flaky dogs, to use the e-collar to force them down a long narrow channel of water. Under the right circumstances, saying "Back" to a dog while she is in motion, and nicking with the collar, can be a good way of reducing pops (stopping to look for help when the whistle was not blown) and spins (spinning around nervously in place rather than progressing steadily towards the objective). With the majority of dogs, however, we keep most of the training pressure "behind the line" rather than on the way to the dummies. If a dog goes a little way and then "breaks down," or refuses a water entry, however, often running after her, stick in hand, will get her going again. If your dog is so unwise as to let you catch her in this circumstance, take hold of her check cord and repeat the "Back-back-back" sequence with the stick. We do all forcing on back with dummies rather than birds in order to keep the conditions more controlled.

When forcing on back is complete, your dog should be reliably free of "no-goes." Just as important, however, her work should also show a noticeable improvement in style and confidence, the result of her knowing clearly what is expected and understanding that you, her handler, will back up your commands. From now on, insist on the standard of reliability you have taught. Back it up with the training stick or e-collar as necessary.

MITCH

M ITCH WAS A VERY HARD-GOING LABRADOR RETRIEVER. What he lacked in brain power he made up for in drive and determination. When compared to many of the smarter dogs I have trained, he was on the low end of the scale. Mitch lacked the ability that many dogs have to make sense out of a new situation. His mission while hunting or field trialing was to get to his objective, as quickly as possible, come hell or high water.

Labradors often have "deep drive." Whether they are very fast or somewhat slow does not necessarily correlate to the quality of drive. Some slower dogs have enough drive to carry them through, and some fast dogs lack it. Many quick, high-energy dogs are superficially flashy. In general, though, the brisk movers exhibit more drive than the "plugs," who are sometimes just lazy. Mitch was both very fast and blessed with deep drive.

From the time I started training Mitch as a four-month-old puppy, no ditch was too deep, no water too wide, nor cover too rough for him to approach with absolute confidence and the range to get the job done. His desire for birds was unsurpassed, and it expressed itself, at times, in a pretty rough mouth. On one occasion, when returning at his usual dead run with a pigeon, he bit down so hard on the bird when he was about 20 feet from me, that the bird's heart popped out of its breast and rolled across the ground.

Mitch was not a hard-mouthed dog. He was merely carried away with the excitement of the moment. I didn't embark on a program to prevent future instances of mishandling the bird. I simply gave a firm reprimand in the event he became overly enthusiastic with his birds. As he got older, the problem disappeared. Mitch never had a mouth problem in hunting or at field trials.

Training a young prospect with an overabundance of drive but limited brain power is a challenging project. You know you have a good dog who will do the work, but are unable to get even some of the simpler concepts across. It was this way with Mitch. Though he would hit the water like dynamite and never shirk a long swim, when he picked up a mark on land across the water, he didn't seem to be able to figure out how to get back. One day, in spite of my usual adherence to our own recommendation of short training sessions, we spent 45 minutes trying to teach Mitch to come back across the water from the far shore, a distance of 40 yards. We used ropes to pull him back, employed a helper to haze him back into the water, and tried other methods of force to try to get Mitch to come straight back. Nothing worked for a long time until the light finally came on and he jumped in the water and came back. One of the advantages of dogs like Mitch is that once they finally learn something, you generally don't have to repeat the lesson. It's getting the message across in the first place that's tough.

Steadiness was another obstacle to surmount. In Mitch's mind, the sight of a bird or a dummy in the air was the signal to take off. We tried various methods to steady him, including the training stick, electric collar, short breaking cord, and so forth. Nothing seemed to delay his explosive departure the instant the retrieving object was sighted. It was difficult to teach marking to Mitch because he was so active on the line that precise marking was impossible.

Finally, we tried the last resort — the rat shot pistol. This won't injure the dog when it is used more than ten yards away. It hurts, though, and will usually stop the breaking. The rat shot technique worked on Mitch. We don't recommend this method any more, as shooting too close can embed shot in your dog's skin. Worse, if your timing is bad, and your dog turns around, you can put out an eye. Many of the training techniques used 20 or 30 years ago have fallen into disuse because of their inherent risks.

Mitch became very steady, and I devised a method of running him in competition that enabled him to bring his marking and memory abilities to a high level. I heeled him to the line on a marking test and commanded him to sit, then stepped back about two steps, allowing Mitch a full view of the guns in the field. I never pointed out gunning stations to Mitch. He could find them on his own. With me behind him, he was never sure that I was not going to reinforce steadiness.

Mitch was blessed with excellent eyes. I'm convinced that he could see better than a man with 20/20 vision. He could pick out a bird in flight in bad light, or objects on the water at extreme ranges. Many dogs have trouble seeing a red retrieving dummy under any circumstances. Mitch was able to spot them at great distances, and would often appear to pick them out at distances of over 200 yards across water. An old timer once said, "What a dog gives up on one end they gain on the other." He was referring to hips. The idea was that if a dog had hip dysplasia, he would make up for it by brainpower, nose, or eyesight. Mitch's hips were radiographically bad, as was true of his siblings that I knew of, but it never slowed him down. He was still going hard when he died at 14.

When I tried to teach Mitch to handle I was apparently up against a "mission impossible." His lining training was laboriously developed with mowed patterns, which he grasped readily, but seemed dependent upon. The jump from a formal pattern to a blind in the field, or worse, in the water, seemed unattainable. The school blinds (those which had been previously taught) he could do. Anything new, he drew a blank and gave me "no-goes." I did not understand forcing on back as well at that time as I do now, and I struggled fruitlessly trying to get Mitch to line to a bird or dummy that he had not seen thrown.

Mitch's problems with lining were largely solved during a training trip to New Jersey. A group of friends and I were alternating throwing the long bird on a difficult marking test from a small island in a pond. When my turn came to throw from the island, I took Mitch with me and made him sit and stay while I threw birds for the other dogs. The mark was so demanding that frequently I had to help a dog by saying "Hey, hey!" and throwing another bird. In these cases, when the running dog finished the test, several minutes after I had thrown the mark, I lined Mitch to the remaining bird. For some reason, this worked, and Mitch started lining to things he had not seen thrown. Why some of these off-beat efforts produce results I don't know, but occasionally they do.

Mitch's first duck hunt was on the coast of North Carolina in Pamlico Sound. The day was windy and cold and we had about 100 diver decoys in our setup off Pamlico Point. Mitch's first retrieve was a 100-yard blind paralleling the shore inside the spread of decoys. He was totally confused. It was puppyhood all over. We struggled with the blind, hacking the dog back and forth. Finally I got out of the boat and walked down the shore to show Mitch the bird. The second retrieve went better, and the third one was very good. Even though Mitch had been through decoys many times in training, this setup of 100 decoys threw him for a loop.

As Mitch grew older, his slowness to learn faded from my

memory, and his brilliance as a performer, both in the hunting field and in formal events, became his hallmark. Mitch finished life as a fine hunting dog and a State Champion gun dog. He also succeeded in field trials. He was known on paper as FC Penney's Nifty Bouncer.

CHAPTER 8

MARKING

A S YOUR PUPPY APPROACHES PHYSICAL MATURITY, you will want to introduce increasingly sophisticated marking concepts and greater range. These challenges should always be presented in a gradual step-by-step manner such as you have used for obedience and yard work. Gradual escalation of difficulty and a thorough understanding of each step are essential. Again, the sessions need not be long. Five to ten minutes is a generous allotment for a marking lesson. Much more than that, particularly if your dog must be called back or otherwise corrected, is apt to sour the dog. A dog in down spirits does not mark at his best.

Up to now, your puppy, depending on his drive, talent, and tractability, will have been doing simple singles. Distances of about 100 yards or so in short cover on land are typical, and maybe half that distance across obvious non-cheating water situations. When your dog has reached the point where he's an ace at that, it's time to move on.

Your puppy will have progressed to the stage by four to six months, depending on individual talent and drive, at which he should have mostly dummies and birds thrown by a bird thrower accompanied by a shot from a blank pistol. The direction and length of these throws is quite important as your dog should mark the bird or dummy with a minimum of dependence on the gunner as a point of reference. Needless to say, bright dogs will always use the guns in the field as marking aids, but it is a good idea to help your puppy to learn to mark the mark, not the gun. It is generally held, and we concur, that the best marks are thrown "flat;" that is, at right angles from the thrower in relationship to a line drawn from the thrower to the dog handler. This encourages the dog to fix his attention on the fall, developing the ability to go directly there.

It used to be argued that a 45° angled back throw was best because it had some of the ingredients of the flat throw and also developed a dog's momentum to carry past the guns. There is some merit to this argument, particularly with dogs who tend to hunt short.

The angled-in throw is very difficult because a young dog with lots of drive will tend to "blow through" such a mark and hunt too deep. Once a dog has gone deep on a mark, it's difficult for him to realize that he must come back to reach his objective.

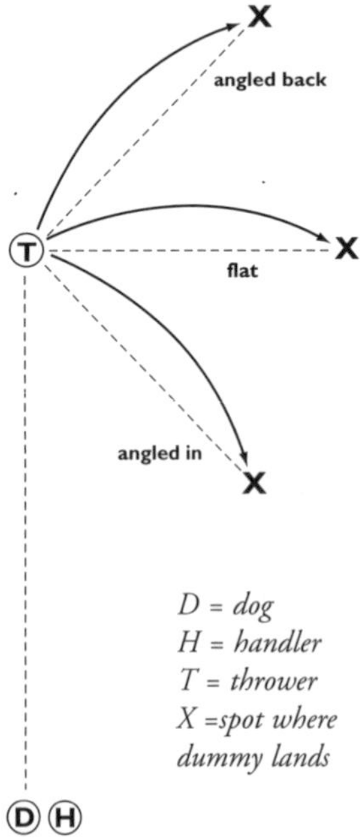

angled back

flat

angled in

D = dog
H = handler
T = thrower
X = spot where
dummy lands

"flat," "angled-back," and "angled-in" throws relative to the dog's vantage point. Throws should always have plenty of arc for good visibility.

Wind Direction and Marking

Wind is a factor in marking. Each type of wind direction relative to the mark presents a unique problem in marking and bird recovery, which must be practiced. A dog's natural tendency is to fade with the wind. Most of them dislike running into the wind. If your thrower is throwing directly down wind, and at right angles to the handler, the dog will tend to drift with the wind to some degree thereby plac-ing himself downwind and in a good position to wind the dummy or bird. However, if the dog drifts too severely down wind, he will often be unsure if he is winding the bird or the bird thrower's station. Practice on the right-angle throw will tend to smooth out a dog's inclination to drift too far with the wind, as experience teaches him that going directly to the mark is more productive.

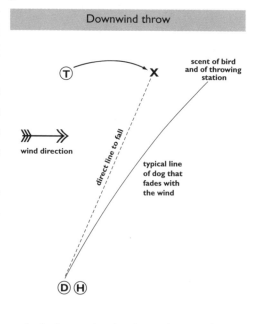

The reverse of the downwind throw is the into-the-wind throw in which the retrieving object is thrown, again, at right angles to the handler, but directly into the wind. The dog's ten-dency here is also to fade down wind, often putting him behind the guns in relationship to the throw. On long and difficult marks this is especially a problem since the dog may forget which side of the thrower the bird is on and become confused by the scent coming off the bird thrower's station. Throw these into-the-wind throws wide and flat to decrease both the natural fad-

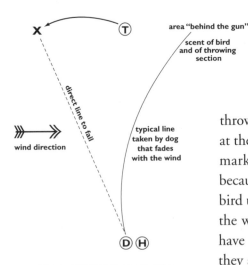

Into-the-wind throw

X

T

area "behind the gun"

scent of bird
and of throwing
section

direct line to fall

wind direction

typical line
taken by dog
that fades
with the wind

D H

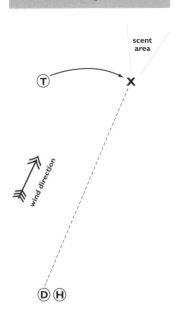

**Mark thrown with wind
at the dog's back**

scent
area

T

X

wind direction

D H

ing with the wind and the tendency to go behind the guns. Keep these marks short at first to increase the likelihood of success.

Next, consider the throw that has the wind directly at the dog's back as he runs to the mark. This mark is difficult because the dog never winds the bird until he has run past it and if the wind is light, many dogs will have trouble "making game" once they are too deep.

The last wind direction in marking practice, and possibly least used although it is important, is the throw that puts the wind off the bird directly in the dog's face. Several problems make this a challenging situation. Dogs' natural reluctance to run into the wind makes them tend to hunt short. If a dog does carry well, and misses the bird on either side, he is apt to go deep, getting into a position where he cannot wind the bird without hunting back in the direction from which he was sent.

Quartering winds and variable winds are common, and they present a mixture of the problems encountered

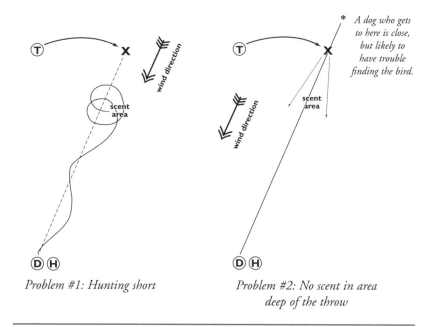

wind direction

scent area

* A dog who gets to here is close, but likely to have trouble finding the bird.

scent area

wind direction

Problem #1: Hunting short

Problem #2: No scent in area deep of the throw

in the four primary wind directions. As a rule of thumb, keep your throws more or less flat and fairly long in order to develop precision marking under all wind conditions.

Range and Cover

As your dog builds confidence in his ability to mark well, no matter what the wind is doing, you will want to extend his range. We often throw marks with white dummies to the limit of a puppy's ability to make the retrieve with enthusiasm and precision. Many puppies of 4 or 5 months of age are able to do retrieves of 100 yards or more under such conditions. When you introduce your puppy to marks in fields with sufficient cover to obscure the bird or dummy, however, you must be careful to limit the distance in order to achieve a high level of success.

If you find your youngster is having nonproductive or rambling hunts, have your thrower help him with a "Hey! hey!", or walk slowly toward the bird, or throw another dummy. Don't let your dog fail. Success builds success in marking. When failure strikes, simplify. A good way to make a mark easier is to move closer to the thrower, or to get on higher ground to improve visibility of the fall. Walk closer to the thrower and call for another throw to land exactly where the first one fell. Make your next marking session easier. Set up shorter marks, and use the wind to your dog's favor. Try to create situations in which he can be successful.

Nobody can say how far a dog can mark. Some top performers seem to be able to mark out to 400 yards or so. Excellent eyes are necessary for this. Others mark well only to 75 or 100 yards. We have long believed that some dogs are near-sighted. This feature of vision does not bear directly on the eye disorders for which dogs are tested by ophthalmologists for CERF certification, such as cataracts, retinal dysplasia, and progressive retinal atrophy. These disorders, too, can adversely affect a dog's visual acuity. You will be able to tell how well your dog sees, provided he has sufficient drive, by gradually extending his marks until you can see that his ears don't come up attentively as he looks in the direction of a thrown bird or dummy.

Keep your marking practice within a range at which your dog can see the throw clearly. Your thrower, particularly at longer ranges, should wear a white shirt or jacket so that the dog has a good opportunity to pick out the location from where the mark will be thrown. Marking that is independent of the thrower can later be taught by the use of retired guns, but for now, keep it as obvious and simple as possible. The throw should also be visible against the background. This may mean that it must be thrown high, so it shows clearly against the sky for part of its flight, or that a different color dummy must be used. Keep in mind that lighting conditions may make it hard to see a gun station even when it contrasts with the background. If you wear a cap or sunglasses to protect your eyes from direct sunlight, remember that your dog must contend with the glare of the sun.

The cover and terrain a dog must negotiate on the way to a mark is an area of primary consideration. The longer the period of time your dog is in high cover (shoulder high or higher), the more chance there is for him to become disoriented. Start out with relatively short (40 to 50 yard) marks in high cover and extend your dog's range gradually as he demonstrates proficiency. Cover can do various things to a dog's marking accuracy besides making visual references harder to maintain. Some cover is physically punishing, hard to get through, and occasionally dangerous. Briars, thickets, sand burrs, and other vegetative barriers range from being somewhat annoying to the dog to being nearly impossible to penetrate. We leave the impenetrable jungles and briar thickets to the "breaks of the game" in the hunting field and field trials. If they occur in those situations, there is little you can do about it. Training through these obstacles on a regular basis invites discouragement, and lessens your dog's abilities and drive in the marking field.

Fields that have changes of cover — strips of plowing alternating with standing

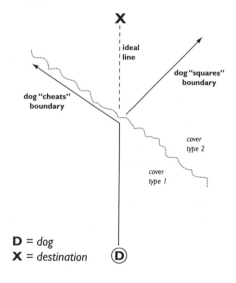

"Cheating" and "squaring" a boundary between two different kinds of cover

D = dog
X = destination

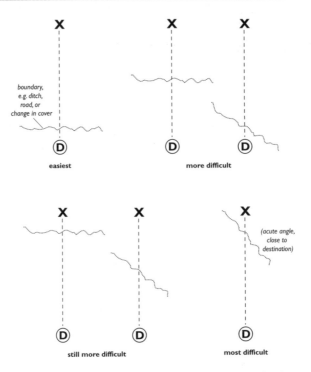

The farther the boundary is from the line (the closer to the destination)
and the more acute the angle, the more difficult it is for the dog to
negotiate correctly. Start simple and work up.

crops, ditches full of high grass or cattails, field roads with
hedgerow growth on either side, etc. — must all be practiced in
order to train a top marking dog. Dogs tend to see a change of
cover as a boundary, and the unschooled dog tends to "square"
these boundaries by turning to cross them at right angles, or to
fail to cross them altogether. The farther out the change of cover,
the more confusing. Start out close to these changes of cover and
work straight across. Then work toward addressing cover changes

at increasingly acute angles, calling your dog back and moving up closer to the cover change if he should try to cheat (run around them). Since you have not trained your dog to handle at this point, you must rely on the call-back, the reprimand, and moving up to improve his performance.

It is important to the development of your marking prospect that during training sessions with other people and their dogs you avoid competition. Work your dog at his own level and his own pace and your dog will gain skills on a gradual basis. Alter the tests that are being run in these groups to accommodate the learning needs of your individual.

Water Marking Practice

The same principles of marking development that apply to land work also apply to water retrieves. Water, however, being a less natural element for the dog, requires additional thought and judgment when setting up marking tests. Water and land work can proceed in parallel or, depending on the season, you may emphasize one first, then catch up on the other.

A dog's range in the water is naturally much shorter than on land. A dog is often capable of covering hundreds of yards on land in less than a minute, with much less expenditure of time and energy than a 75-yard swim. As a result, it pays to keep the water work shorter, at least to start with, and stay close to or under your 10-minute training session time. Achieving proficiency at water marking is an even more gradual process than developing land marking skills. Of course, some dogs have much greater abilities in the water than others, so your starting point and rate of progress need to be based on what your particular dog can do.

Early in your puppy's water work you should have taught only direct entries into shallow water with gradual deepening and no temptation to cheat. The same principles should apply as you advance your dog. Complicated entries, points, islands, tough cover, and other difficult circumstances can gradually be added as he matures.

Since a dog's eyes, while swimming, are on the same level as a bird or dummy floating in the water, his depth perception is severely limited. This factor necessitates your dog's learning to carry a good line in the water so that he will nearly bump into his objective. Dogs will take cues from stumps, clumps of grass, trees and other objects on the shore or in the water, using them as points of reference on these marks as they learn to carry a straight line to the objective. In field trials, remembering what side of the boat a duck was thrown on and other such cues are of great help. Perhaps the most difficult water mark is the long mark thrown into an expanse of open water, especially if the duck is waterlogged and mostly sunken. Here, the dog has nothing to go by but memory and dead reckoning. It is exciting to watch a dog execute such a mark brilliantly. It is indeed a rare talent.

Your first mission in improving your dog's water marks is to increase his range. If your puppy has been going 30 yards in the water, lengthen the distance to 50 until he does that well, then 75 and so on until you have reached the limits of his abilities and ambition. Later, when your dog is fully forced, and handling, you can extend these marking ranges to whatever distance you deem feasible. We note here — do not underestimate the distance at which waterfowl can fall after being mortally wounded. As John found out many years ago from a close friend who learned the trick from his father, whenever you shoot at a bird, watch it until it has flown out of sight. Many ducks and geese who have received a shotgun pellet in the lungs, liver, or other internal organs may fly great distances, and then fold up in mid-flight several hundred yards away, falling dead on the water. A good marking dog may mark these birds at distances as much as several hundred yards on a good day, and make a beautiful retrieve.

A V-shaped pond is excellent for extending your dog's marking range because you are able to apply gradual increments in distance while keeping the dog on familiar water. You may start at the beginning of the month with a 40 to 50 yard retrieve and arrive at the wide end of the pond with a 150-yard mark at the end of the month. Be sure to spend a few days at each distance until your dog is confident and successful. Throw the dummies in the edge of the water and make them white for now. Cover and hidden marks can be introduced after your dog has the range. Get the range first. Avoid cheating temptations until you have taught your dog to go straight, as described in Chapter 7.

As your puppy gains proficiency in the open water, you can introduce him to marks in water with vegetation (cattails, tules, lily pads, and tree stumps). Decoys can be added at this time, too. Bear in mind that since navigation in water is more difficult than on land, distance and other difficulties must be limited until your dog demonstrates that he can handle the challenges. If you have been blessed, however, with one of those geniuses who really comes to life in the water, take advantage of his talent. Capitalize on it!

Maintain Standards and Discipline

Expect your dog's steadiness, line manners, and delivery to show signs of deterioration as you progress into the area of marking at the higher levels. Don't be content to let that happen. If you do, it will be a short time until your earlier work will be undone. Usually, you will have a harder time reteaching work that is undone than you had teaching it the first time. It is better to maintain the standards of performance your dog has learned, even if this necessitates working on simpler marks, than to be inconsistent in your requirements.

It is a good idea when introducing shot birds to your trainee to be especially on guard for the development of bad habits. If your dog creeps (moves at all) or breaks (goes without being sent) make your training stick or slingshot correction on the rump, have your thrower pick up the bird, and start over. It's a long time until a dog is really steady, and some need occasional reminders throughout their lives. Most high-drive dogs will break from time to time, but for the most part, it can be controlled. Creeping (moving a few feet or more toward the downed bird without actually breaking) is another matter. Most dogs that do this will creep to some extent on every bird, at least every shot flier, and as a rule, it only gets worse. Live with it if you must, but living without it is a lot more pleasant, and dogs that don't creep generally mark better.

If your dog begins to mishandle birds or bumpers during his marking training, take him off marks for a few days or a week and return to the force fetching program. Your attention to manners and delivery will pay lifelong dividends as he will become an adult with well-formed habits, having forgotten such adolescent activities as breaking, creeping, and poor delivery.

Walking marks are an excellent procedure for getting your young dog to mark independently and well. It is also a good way to brush up sloppy marking in an older dog. Five or six difficult marks, land or water, are usually sufficient for a ten-minute workout. You can trade off throwing duties with your training partner. When working more than one dog, we usually use red surveyor's flags to mark the locations of the falls in order to prevent the confusion of too many different scent spots in the field. It is a good idea to alternate the direction of the throws and to move 30 to 50 yards between throws in order to avoid the confusion of overlapping areas. We like to give walking marks to puppies almost every day and increase the number according to the ability and energy of the student.

Double Marked Retrieves or "Doubles"

At some point, when your young dog is doing so well on his singles that you can't wait to try something more advanced, you are ready for the introduction of doubles. We always start this as a "schooled double," that is, by employing a single, or a mark that the dog has already practiced, and then throw another dummy as a diversion. All of the marks that your pup has learned during earlier training can then be employed as "starter" memory birds. Your dog will catch on more quickly if you keep things familiar in this way. A "diversion" is simply a shorter mark that is thrown after a longer mark. The diversion is retrieved first thereby making the first throw a "memory bird." For these initial doubles, the diversion is thrown "off-line," that is, by the handler or someone standing close by.

If you are involved with AKC or NAHRA hunting tests, you may have heard the term "diversion" used differently. Unfortunately, the organizers of these programs assigned the

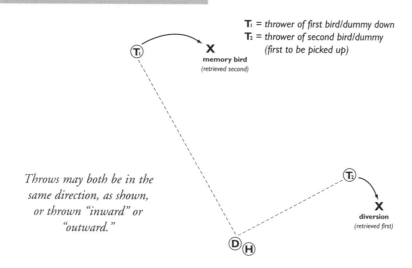

Standard setup for a double mark

T₁ = thrower of first bird/dummy down
T₂ = thrower of second bird/dummy
(first to be picked up)

X
memory bird
(retrieved second)

Throws may both be in the same direction, as shown, or thrown "inward" or "outward."

X
diversion
(retrieved first)

word "diversion" to refer to a more complicated routine traditionally known as a "bulldog" mark, which is a mark thrown for the dog as he is on his way in with another mark. He must, of course, continue with the bird he has and not switch. As used in this book, however, "diversion" has its traditional meaning of a mark that is picked up first, diverting the dog's attention from the memory mark, or first mark thrown.

When the dog is doing well with only one thrower in the field and a diversion throw off line, he is ready for two gunners in the field. Keep them wide spread. 180° is not necessary, but 90° or so is advisable. Run each mark as a single and continue to do this for quite a while (a few weeks) until he expects to be sent on the single. This keeps his attention riveted on the first mark thrown and helps to prevent that dread malady — "head swinging." Head swinging is a problem in which the dog does not watch the first bird fully down but swings his head to look at the second thrower in anticipation of the second mark. It can be especially pronounced when the second mark is to be a shot flier. During the course of your work on doubles, if your dog should begin to swing his head away from the first throw, don't call for the second throw, but re-heel your dog and send him for the first mark. Some pretty severe cases of head-swinging have been effectively treated in this way. Notice that this treatment works only if you, the handler, cue each of your throwers separately — a good practice in general.

As an additional feature in doubles marking, you can introduce variations in the order of the throws. To start with, the second bird down should be the closer of the two marks, and the first picked up. Gradually, you can introduce throws at about the same distance but still at least 90° apart. Vary the order — right `first, left second on one day, then left first, right second on the next. In different sessions and locations, vary the directions of the throws: both to the right, both to the left, together (pincer), and apart (mama & papa). Do not run different tests in the same area in the same or consecutive sessions, though, as your dog's memory of the birds he has already retrieved is likely to confuse him. As you vary the directions and distance of throws, your dog will learn to mark the individual mark and remember the memory bird. If marks are thrown according to a rigid pattern, he will become habituated to that pattern and will be easily fooled by change.

Keep in mind that your marking sessions must be kept short. The stress of corrections, repetition, rough going and long swims quickly take their toll on a dog's enthusiasm. Work progressively and keep your sessions separated by a few hours even on those weekend training days when you want to get a lot done.

Out-of Order Marks

As your pupil progresses in proficiency, by virtue of a gradual and relaxed program, you will reach a point at which variations in the order and proximity of marks, previously avoided, will become beneficial. Until now, your youngster has had a variety of marks thrown in different directions. These marks have been reasonably wide-spread and predominantly thrown in the traditional order, i.e. longer throw first, shorter throw second. What happens when, out of the blue, you throw the short mark first followed by the long one second? Don't do it. Sure, your dog might run out to the long one, pin it, come back and ace the short one, or he might turn around and go for the short throw first, do a good job there, then go after the long mark (second one down) and do a fine job. More likely, your youngster will take a line for the last mark down, the long one, change his mind and head for the shorter mark ending up between the two, in no-man's land, failing both marks.

There is a way you can train for these "out-of-order" throws and at the same time prepare your trainee for secondary selection (a procedure in which the shorter memory bird in a triple is retrieved second, usually after the flier, which is shot down last and retrieved first). We teach this by first throwing a double in the conventional manner: long first, short second. We then repeat the test, throwing the birds in the reverse order. Most young dogs will automatically turn from the long bird and go for the short bird even though it was not the last one down. If this is practiced without pressure and through gentle repetition, your dog will learn to mark in a relaxed and positive fashion and not be overburdened with an excess of principles as to how a mark "should be done." Bear in mind that marking, even in complex setups, is natural behavior enhanced by training, not arrived at through heavy corrections.

Switching and returning to old falls are undesirable in hunting as well as in field trials (in which your dog will be eliminated). When your dog indicates a mark while at your side and you send him in that direction, you want him to go straight to the destination you have both agreed upon, and not to change his mind and head somewhere else. It is important to train in a manner that consistently reinforces this continuity of purpose. When your dog is taking hand signals, these failures can be corrected by stopping your dog and handling, but you will be ahead of the game if you can establish these principles in your puppy. This can be done by helping your youngster to the mark he is failing with a "Hey, hey!" from the thrower, then repeating. Usually the bright student will learn from help and will not develop a fear of marking tests. Punishing these failures, on the other hand, can make your dog a worried and ineffective marker.

Tight marks — marks that are close together in either angle or actual distance — must be introduced gradually. If you find that you are falling significantly below the 75 percent success level, ease up on the difficulty. Increase the angle and when you reestablish your dog's confidence, begin to tighten them up again. Remember, you can never go wrong by giving your dog a break. If he has the necessary desire, he wants to mark and retrieve. It is up to you to present him with a series of marks that are challenging enough to build improvement, but not so stiff as to wipe out his enthusiasm.

A final note on early marking is in order. When a dog misses a mark, switches, returns to old falls, or wanders aimlessly in the wrong area, he is generally less happy with his work than you are. He may act confused, dejected, and lost. You will compound the problem by giving him a good shaking-up for his apparent lack of diligence. This will harm your dog's attitude toward marking, and his proficiency. We have seen cases of such training take a severe toll in a good dog. We have also witnessed cases of dogs so tough and resilient that no amount of abusive training seemed to dampen their enthusiasm for marking, or to interfere with their increasing skill at coming up with the bird. Such cases are extremely rare, though, so avoid the angry blow-up. There are many factors, some of which we have discussed, which can contribute to the difficulty of a marking test. If you throw a set of marks that you expect your dog to do easily but he fails, chances are some unperceived difficulty made it a harder test than you realized. You will never do your dog any harm by assuming this is the case, and by simplifying the test to ensure success.

CRICKET

by John

I fiRST SAW CRICKET WHEN SHE WAS ABOUT THREE-AND-A-half months old. She had been stepped on as a small puppy and had her leg casted for some time, which I think set back her development throughout puppyhood. Her mother, FC-AFC Penney of Evergreen, and her father, FC-AFC Samson's George of Glenspey, were both well bred and excellent dogs, so it was no surprise when Cricket exhibited intense retrieving desire and precise marking ability. Cricket's personality was always a little strange, I thought, as she seemed reluctant to relate to human beings, particularly strangers, of whom she was often shy.

I was working for her owner at the time, doing some late-in-life training with Cricket's mother, Penney, when Cricket was sent off to another person for training. I heard only the sketchiest of reports on Cricket's progress over the next six months, and was quite curious to know how she was developing.

I found out when Cricket was entered in a puppy stake in my home town in North Carolina. The stake was a demanding one, as puppy trials go. It consisted of two land series and a couple of tough water singles. All contestants were allowed to run all of the tests whether they successfully completed the previous series or not. Cricket ran all four series along with a dozen other contestants, but failed to complete any of the retrieves. I was disappointed in her showing because I liked her as a puppy and, as she was approaching her first birthday, I had presumed she would perform well.

Cricket's owner was understandably disappointed in her showing, and took the dog home with the idea of giving up on her field trial career. I still felt that Cricket had promise and offered my services to see if I could bring her around.

Having the opportunity to train Cricket was a mixed blessing. While I maintained faith that she was worth the effort, her response to training was generally so negative that the prospect of her learning to do advanced work was in doubt. She was the type of dog that could not take physical pressure. In those days, the electric collar had one strength — HOT — too hot for Cricket. I couldn't use a training stick on her because she was too fast and she always knew when it was coming. About the only thing that worked on Cricket was the slingshot. I had to conceal it, however, as she seemed to possess a sixth sense concerning anything you might do to her.

Cricket seemed to know if you were angry, no matter how you tried to conceal it. All the "Good girl, c'mon, good girl, tch, tch, tch's" were of no use. She would stand just far enough away so that she could not be caught. During this period, I usually trained her with a 20-foot length of polypropylene cord in order to keep her under wraps.

The up side of working with Cricket was that she was fast, an accurate marker, very birdy, and loved to retrieve. Water marking was her strong suit. I can't remember a field trial in which she made it to the last series without turning in a good performance on the most demanding part of the field trial — the water triple or quadruple.

Before it was feasible to compete with Cricket, it was necessary to teach her to do water blinds. She had run well in the Derby, where blinds are not required, getting several placements. The next step, however, was the Qualifying, in which the water blind is an important part of the trial.

To begin with, Cricket simply would not do a water blind. She had been taught land blinds by the old method of lining up white dummies every ten yards straight out in a field of short grass. She learned her side and back casts without the aid of formal yard patterns. I taught her to stop on a whistle by blowing the whistle and hollering, "Sit!" until she got it — that was it. Cricket picked up these ideas very quickly — on land. It was another matter in the water. I tried sight blinds (confidence blinds built on a mark she had done), but I could not get her to enter the water on a cold blind. She always ran down to the water's edge and disappeared into the bushes, or stopped and refused to continue.

I finally decided to use the electric collar, even though I knew from previous experiments with it that it would most likely overwhelm her. I returned to precisely the same blind I had tried the day before where she had responded by slipping off into the high cover to hide. On this occasion, however, I blew the whistle just as Cricket approached the water, and as she sat, I burned her with a short shock, raised my hand over my head, and hollered, "Back!"

The result was amazing. Cricket turned around with alacrity, jumped into the water, and swam to the end of the pond, approximately 50 yards, to make a perfect retrieve. The next day, I returned to the same place with the intention of repeating the blind. I opened Cricket's box, put the electric collar on her, and before I could get to the line to send her, Cricket took off for the water, bailed in at the same place she entered the day before, and did a perfect water blind.

This training procedure worked, but it did not solve the problem of Cricket's attitude toward water blinds. She always harbored a hatred for that part of her job even though her performances were often good. Once she was wet on a water blind,

Cricket could be counted upon to behave almost perfectly. In competition, however, collars of any kind are not allowed, and the problem of refusals at the point of water entry persisted.

Once again, things were looking grim. It became necessary to resort to the electric collar as a preliminary to any water blind she faced in competition. I had to take Cricket away from the nosy crowd, substantially off the trial grounds, put the collar on her while she was in her box, and give her two shocks with the collar while firmly saying, "Back! Back!" If I did this shortly before her turn to run, I generally got her to do a good blind.

Cricket's other major hang-up was her shyness of strangers, particularly very large men. In an early Qualifying stake, one of the judges was a 250-pounder. When he raised his judging book to signal for the first bird of the land triple, Cricket caught the movement out of the corner of her eye, turned around, and backed off while barking at him. Of course, with her back to the marks, she could not see them being thrown, and was out of the trial — leaving me with another tough problem to solve.

My solution to the shyness problem was very effective. Cricket had a great love for dog treats, little milk bones and such. I went through the gallery at a field trial and asked the biggest men I could find to put a milk bone in their pockets. When I approached them later, with Cricket on lead, I asked them to call her up in a friendly manner and give her a treat. It worked beautifully. After a few repetitions, Cricket became confident enough to overcome her spookiness of strangers.

With two major obstacles to success in competition eliminated, Cricket went on to win and place in licensed field trials. She won two Qualifying stakes rather quickly, and not long afterward was awarded a couple of seconds and a first in the Open All-Age stake to make her field championship. What looked like an impossibility at 11 months of age had become a reality.

Cricket's combination of talent and desire with troubling flaws illustrates a fact about retrievers. Variation among dogs is tremendous, and very few individuals "have it all." Most have at least one flaw: a difficulty in some area, or perhaps an inability to profit by some standard training procedure. The key to a satisfactory outcome begins with accepting the reality of a particular dog's strengths and weaknesses. Being willing to depart from training dogma to seek a creative, tailored solution may make the difference between a valued hunting or competition dog and a washout. Accepting that your dog, in all probability, has some limitations may make the difference between being satisfied with him or her, or being gravely disappointed.

CHAPTER 9

A BRIEF INTRODUCTION TO HANDLING

W E HAVE TRIED TO SET FORTH A PROGRAM of training that will enable the reader to accomplish most facets of retriever work without the aid of hand signals. Blind retrieves, of course, require handling. Selection (sending your dog for a specific bird) and honesty training (de-cheating) are also enhanced by the use of hand signals. Once your retriever will handle, you are in a position to show her the line you want her to take.

If you have trained your dog according to the steps outlined in this book, you should now be ready to introduce directional hand signals. The groundwork has been laid — your dog is force fetched, forced-on-back both on land and water, and will sit when you blow a single blast on the whistle. The only remaining job is to teach her to cast: run or swim in the direction of your hand signals.

The key to teaching handling, or casting as it is often called, is simplicity and repetition. Most retrievers seem to have a natural affinity for following the directions in which you wave your arms, particularly lateral directions. Casts away from you (back) are more difficult and will require more emphasis than the "overs," or lateral casts. Proficient handling retrievers should also know how to cast in (toward you) in the event they should over-run their objective. Since the force-on-back procedure has been the most arduously taught of a retriever's lessons, the come-in cast is often surprisingly difficult to accomplish, especially at long distances.

In order to begin teaching your pupil to handle, place her in a sit-stay half way out to the pile of dummies you have been using for the force-on-back program. This will put her about 35-40 yards from you, and an equal distance from the pile of dummies. Blow your whistle once to establish attention. This should remind your dog that she is to remain sitting, facing you. Wait a couple of seconds, then raise a hand straight over your shoulder at full extension and command, "Back!"

Most dogs who have already learned the pile location during forcing on back will pick this up quickly and run back to get a dummy. If your dog acts balky or confused, move closer to her until she spins around on the back command and makes a retrieve from the pile. If necessary, toss another dummy on the pile to give her the idea. You want your dog to turn to your right when you cast with your right arm, and to your left when you cast with your left arm. If necessary, stand a little to one side or the other to help her get the right idea.

In between back casts to the pile of dummies, return your dog to the sending line and send her from your side on the back command just as you did during your forcing-on-back. Spend a few days practicing this until your dog acts confident and shows signs of enthusiasm. If she is anxious or apprehensive you are not ready to move on. When the foregoing has been mastered, we repeat the same lesson only with side casts (over) to a pile of dummies about 20 yards to the right and left of her sitting position halfway to the back pile. You can remove the dummies at the back pile so

"Back" cast

"Over" cast

"Come-in" cast

"Angle back" cast

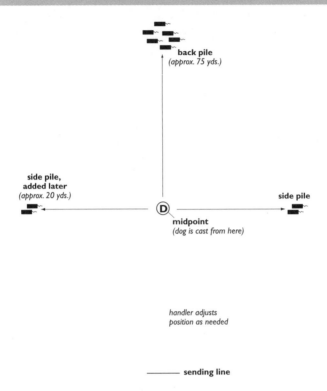

back pile
(approx. 75 yds.)

side pile,
added later
(approx. 20 yds.)

side pile

(D)

midpoint
(dog is cast from here)

*handler adjusts
position as needed*

——— sending line

your dog will not be tempted to run back to that pile while you are trying to teach side casts, or leave them in place. Usually, the presence of the "back" pile presents minimal difficulty when teaching "overs."

Always blow your single blast on the whistle before giving a cast, even though your dog is already in the sitting position. She must be looking at you attentively before a hand signal is given. If your dog's attention wanders, blow a sharp tweet-tweet-tweet come-in whistle and as soon as she starts to move toward you, blow the single blast sit whistle. This should reestablish eye contact. A dog who will not watch the handler during this stage of training cannot be taught to handle well. A dog that does not look at you to handle, deliberately turning her head away and avoiding eye contact, is either bored, confused, or both. In any case, she is avoiding the issue. If this happens, back up to an earlier step, make the sessions briefer, and reestablish confidence and enthusiasm.

After you have taught your dog to take back casts, lateral casts, and a come-in cast (put a dummy halfway between yourself and your dog, and blow a come-in whistle) you are ready to put dummies at all three major stations: back, left over, and right over. Occasionally you can put one in the come-in position as well. Now, select the pile you want your dog to go to, and cast to it. The back cast should be practiced most, about three times as often as all of the others put together. Most dogs have a greater tendency to run to a side pile than to get back, so back must be more heavily stressed. If your dog makes a mistake, immediately blow the sit whistle, move closer, and repeat the cast until you succeed. Don't let her carry through to a complete retrieve on a casting error. If this should happen, run to her, take the dummy quickly from her mouth while saying, "No, no," throw that dummy back to its pile, and resume casting your dog to your original objective. A lot of correction is not required here, although indirect pressure in the sitting position — sit-nick-sit with the e-collar — often restores attentiveness and discipline. If you attempt to apply direct pressure with the collar while your dog is on the move, she will most likely run to the back pile because of her earlier training on forcing back.

It is hard to suggest a time frame for this first stage of handling education. Stay with each lesson until your dog does it smoothly. Most dogs can learn to handle on a yard pattern (single or double T) in a matter of weeks.

Combining Lining, Stopping on the Whistle, and Casting

When your dog is watching attentively and casting smoothly in all directions with no hangups and few errors, you are ready to combine lining, stopping on the whistle, and casting. Your dog has mastered all of these skills separately, and it only remains to put them together.

Return to your sending point (line) 75 yards from the back pile with no side dummies out. Send your dog with the "Back" command. When she reaches the halfway point blow the sit whistle. If she does not sit facing you, blow a come-in, and then another sit whistle, to get her facing you. Next, give a straight up back cast with either arm. If your dog turns to your left on a right-hand cast, immediately blow the whistle and get her to sit facing you, then repeat the cast. It is important to insist that she turn in the direction of the arm you use, even though the wrong turn may appear harmless at this point. Later, when she is handling at greater distances, the value of having her turn in the proper direction will become vividly apparent.

About half to three-quarters of the time, line "through" to the pile with no sit whistle, as you will want your dog to understand that no whistle means "keep going." If your dog pops (looks back at the intersection), as she is likely to do in the beginning, do not blow the whistle. Just raise your hand while moving quickly toward her and repeat "Back" in a commanding tone.

When your dog will go on command, will stop promptly on the whistle to sit facing you, and will cast back turning in the correct direction, you are ready to add lateral casts. Follow the same procedure as on the back casts, only cast her to the right or left after making her sit halfway out. Mix in back casts and sends where you line your dog through without stopping, in whatever proportion necessary to keep getting straight back uppermost in her mind. Re-casts will become necessary as your dog elects to go to whatever pile strikes her fancy — usually one of the side piles. Persist. Every time your dog makes a mistake, make her sit and repeat the cast. She will soon give up cast refusals when you convince her that going in a direction other than that of your cast is nonproductive.

Most dogs enjoy the handling pattern and seem to view it as a game. If you keep the fun aspect at a fairly high level, you are apt to produce a dog that not only lines and handles precisely, but does so with verve and style. This does not mean you must "rev up" your dog with "freebies" and high-pitched chatter — but do continue to keep sessions short and adjust the level of challenge so she is successful most of the time.

Your responsibility in teaching handling is clarity. Practice giving proper casts in a mirror. Over casts should be absolutely lateral, not pointing toward or away from the dog. Back casts should be straight up. Give your dog the benefit of maximum visibility. Wear a white shirt while training and she will be better able to see your casts. Be careful about placing your other hand on your hip, or using it to shade your eyes — this presents a confusing picture. Hunting tests require handlers to wear camo at their events, but in many settings, a cast given while wearing camo, with foliage as a backdrop, cannot be seen by the dog. In training, before your dog fully understands, it is crucial to make your casts as clearly visible as possible.

To add the come-in cast on the pattern, send your dog up the middle with dummies at all three stations. Before she arrives at the usual sitting station, throw a dummy inconspicuously toward her (preferably a hard-to-see orange or black one), then blow the sit whistle. This should be followed by a come-in whistle with your hands down by your side. Your dog can then pick up the dummy on her way back to you.

When your dog demonstrates the ability to execute the handling pattern in the yard for a dozen or so straight training ses-

Incorrect casts

sions, you are ready to take her to the field. Most dogs show considerable confusion on their first effort to run a blind away from the yard pattern. You can prepare your dog for this by establishing a few confidence or "school" blinds, which you teach by identifying the location of the dummies to her first. Most retrievers remember blind locations well, and a couple of exposures to blinds in known locations should enable your dog to line them, even at distances of 200 yards and more. Next, you can stop her at any point in her progress toward these school blinds and give your most used cast, the back, to the dummy.

When you can return to the location of any of your school blinds and run them smoothly, you are ready to introduce "cold" blinds to your dog. Bear in mind that the cold blind — one which the dog does not know — is a big jump. It should bear a strong resemblance to the school blinds you have been doing, only in a new place. Using large white dummies placed in short cover or in other places where they are visible from some distance helps insure that your dog will be rewarded for starting out willingly and "staying with you" through a number of casts. On these early blind retrieves, concentrate on getting your dog to the objective. Do not pick at her with numerous casts intended to keep her "on line." Good lines will come later; for now, if a cast is carrying your dog closer to the destination, get as much distance out of it as possible. This will aid development of range, confidence, and the ability to carry a cast.

As a retriever progresses in her blind work, a variety of conditions, such as changes of cover or going in and out of more than one piece of water, can be introduced. Try to teach your dog a set of familiar "pictures," and the appropriate response for each. For example, if there is water in the distance and you send her at it, she will expect to get in. If you line her at a channel, she will know to swim up the middle. If you send her at a point or island, she will expect to cast back into the water on the far side. If at a ditch or change of cover, she will know how to hold her line. These desired responses are all counter to dogs' "natural" tendencies in each situation, so each one will require patient teaching and plenty of practice. Once your dog understands a blind retrieve as a sequence of "pictures," she will be able to negotiate them with confidence, even in an unfamiliar setting. You will also neet to teach her to line and cast into the wind. This is difficult for almost all dogs, so again, work patiently.

There is no limit to what you can teach in the realm of lining and handling. Remember to keep each new maneuver clear to your dog, building up complex challenges through a series of steps, rather than hammering it into your dog all in one session. Holding off on heavy correction and relying on attrition (the gradual replacement of behavior you don't want with that you do want) is important to developing a confident, hard-going blind dog. As in pattern training, correction should be administered after you have established control with your dog sitting in an attentive position.

We have found that dogs who receive a lot of heavy correction when they are far out in the field, whether on blinds or marks, become slow, morose, and often do not want to get out of the truck for training sessions. It is far better to move up on your dog, making the cast and correction clearer.

Very few dogs learn to do difficult blind retrieves with consistency before they are two-and-a-half to three years of age. Even then, occasional break-downs and failures can be expected. Always be sure that your dog can see you and hear your whistle, and has the proper preparation for what you are trying to get her to do before applying pressure. Keep the pressure light. We think you will be pleased with your handling retriever as many birds, especially those shot from a duck blind, cannot be seen as marks.

REAL
DOGS

A MAINE DUCK HUNT
by John

IT WAS A BEAUTIFUL, MID-OCTOBER WEEKEND on Montauk
Point, Long Island. The field trial season was in full swing
and, for a change, we weren't overly disappointed to go out
of the trial early. We were eager to get on our way to Buck Bluff,
Maine, for a week of duck hunting. It had been three years since
I left Maine and the wonderful coastal duck hunting that I
enjoyed while I lived there. Nostalgia was calling.

My friend, Ken, my son, Anton, and I had been looking forward to this trip all summer, and we harbored expectations of a
rewarding hunt. When we left our home in North Carolina, the
leaves had barely begun to show color, but by the time we
reached New York, the landscape was resplendent with yellows,
reds, and golds, and the air smelled of Autumn.

We had three Labs along — Ken's Joe, Anton's Midnight, and
my Jade. All three were well trained, proficient retrievers, while
Ken's Joe held an edge on talent in my estimation. We were
rigged with a good boat and blind, about three dozen mallard
and black duck decoys, and were traveling in my relic 1946
International pickup. Being three good-sized guys, we made a
pretty tight fit in the seat of that truck.

Looking like dispossessed farmers from the dust bowls of the
1930s, we made our way across Long Island Sound via the
Riverhead ferry, and from the Connecticut shore Northward on
I-95 to our hunting destination near Buck Bluff, Maine. That
village consisted of a little general store and a half dozen houses—typical of Maine small towns.

Our objective was to hunt Perkins Pond, a beautiful little impoundment of fresh water that emptied directly into Covington's Pond, a tidal marsh. Like many others on the Maine Coast, Covington's Pond varied in water depth from zero to about ten feet, according to the tides.

When we reached the state of Maine, the scenery was quite different than New York's autumn spectacle. Almost all of the leaves had fallen except for a scattering of tenacious beeches, and the trees were a haze of soft gray with a carpet of dull brown leaves beneath them. Clearly, winter was in the offing.

We proceeded to retrace my son's and my steps of three years earlier to find Perkins Pond, a remote little body of water with public access — if you could find it. When we got to the pond, we were devastated to find it practically dry. We walked the shoreline to the dam and found that it had collapsed, possibly from the pressure of tons of ice during previous winters.

Since Covington's Pond was immediately below Perkins, we weren't without a place to hunt and we decided that, since we had a week to make of it, we'd spend the next morning on the small strip of water that remained in our original destination. We pitched camp that night on a small island covered with spruces on Covington's Pond. The ground was deep with a cushion of many years' spruce needles and we scarcely needed any other padding beneath our sleeping bags.

It was dark when we pushed the boat off for shore and Perkin's Pond on the other side of a minor road. We had decided to pack in a small number of decoys and shoot from the edge of the mud flat bordering the water that ran down through the old lake bed. It was a mucky proposition, slogging knee deep in mud for 40 yards to put out decoys. Crossing through the old creek bed was out of the question, except for the dogs, of course.

By the first hint of daylight we were set up and waiting for whatever might fly down the smidgen of water that was left. By the time the sun came up and melted the frost from the grassy edge where we were hiding, we had not seen a duck. I decided to take Jade, leaving my son and Ken, and walk over the hill to the east to see what remained of another part of the lake. There was nothing. The entire lake bed had grown up in sumac, thistles, and wild roses — a dry thicket.

About the time I was ready to return, I heard a barrage of shots from the direction of our blind. I went back to see what was up and both Ken and Anton were flailing away with their arms trying to handle dogs across the mud flat to pick up a couple of greenwing teal. Neither dog wanted to get into that quagmire to retrieve the ducks on the far side of the flat.

Jade, while she was less of a dog in competition or training than either Midnight or Joe, rose to the occasion. I instructed my hunting partners to call in their dogs and proceeded to line up Jade from the top of the hill. She unhesitatingly lined across the expanse of quicksand for one bird, and back again for the other. She was so consistently behind the other two dogs in formal work that I was pleased to see them outdone for a change.

That was Jade's nature. She seemed to be made for hunting, and did many things during her 14 years that struck me as uncanny. Many dog men rationalize their dogs' weaknesses in training or competition by saying, "He may not be much here, but you should see him in the hunting field." Usually this is just hot air; what you see in training or in field trials, you will also see while hunting. Jade was the exception to a rule that has held true with most of the dogs I have trained.

We could see, after that morning, that we were not going to have much success on the trickle of water left in Perkins Pond. We decided to take our operation back to Covington's Pond where we were camped. The move was easy — only a hundred yards to carry the blind and decoys and we were back to our boat, ready to push off.

The tides in many Maine coastal ponds are spectacular. They rush in as a raging torrent and go out the same way. In this particular pond there was a narrow passage for the incoming and outgoing tides not more than 50 yards wide, and the current was so strong there during the peak flow that my Evinrude 5 horse lost headway when I tried to motor upstream through the pass.

There were some permanent blinds constructed on Covington's Pond. At high tide, they would be almost inundated. At low tide they would sit lonely and unsteady spectacles rising some 10 feet above the mud flat. The best hunting from these places was at medium tide. If the water was too high, your boat would be in plain sight above the top of the blind. If the tide was out, you would have a ten-foot blind towering above your boat.

We positioned our boat with its portable blind on the edge of the waterway that coursed through the lake bed, which provided a reasonably good position throughout the day. We had decided to leave two dogs in their boxes on the truck, taking only Jade with us in the boat. Three men and an 80-pound Lab are too much for most boats and our little 14-footer was cramped.

Then I struck on an idea. Jade was an excellent handling dog and would do just about anything you asked of her if she could understand it. I decided to give her a line to a small wooded island about 75 yards from the location of our boat. When she reached the island I commanded, "Jade, sit and stay!"

She complied, and held that position until we shot our first duck. When the duck went down, I hollered, "Jade, back!" and she hit the water, picked up the duck, and brought it to the boat. We didn't have much shooting that day, nor did we during the rest of the week. We got a smattering of teal, gadwall, and maybe a goldeneye or two, but Jade learned to operate from that island almost immediately. She would lie down under the boughs of a cedar tree, basking in the low-angled rays of the sun, and wait for us to shoot. After the second duck, she returned to her roost on the little island without any direction from me to wait for more action. We hunted the rest of the afternoon, getting few shots and fewer birds, but were rewarded by the intelligence and resourcefulness we saw in Jade.

During the hunting on Covington's Pond, my son and I recalled a toy boat that he had whittled out of a pine board, and left at another boat landing on the pond at the end of our previous stay in Maine. The day we left it, the pond was largely frozen over, and when we embarked for the morning's hunt, we had to slide the boat over a 100-yard sheet of ice that sloped down toward the center of the lake. The tide was about half out and the ice formed a slide toward the open water. Anton had left the little wooden boat on the edge of the ice near the shore and we decided to look for it.

We found the home crafted toy almost immediately when we reached the landing site where he had left it. Three years of going in and out with the tides and it was in the same place! We found the fact that the boat was still there hard to believe — certainly not typical of what you see and feel when you try to return to old haunts. Usually, the land is different, the people are different, and you have changed, too. It's never the same. We left the boat there a second time, but have never gone back to look for it.

Note: The names of the Maine town and ponds have been changed out of consideration for those who still hunt there.

CHAPTER 10

FIELD TRIALS & HUNTING TESTS

I T SEEMS THAT ANY ACTIVITY, PARTICULARLY on the American sporting scene, inevitably leads to the development of a competitive event. Shooting contests have been around for well over 100 years, and more recently, contests for all sorts of hunting dogs have received the sanction of various kennel clubs.

Retriever field trials, even though these events are frequently beyond what your dog would be required to do in a "normal" day's hunt, emphasize principles that are generally good. Overkill serves one better than being under-prepared. No one could correctly assert that a dog's ability to execute a 400-yard blind retrieve, after completing a difficult triple mark in the same field, would jeopardize his chances of completing the retrieves in an ordinary shooting situation.

One of the real benefits, perhaps the most important one, of formal retriever events is that they give the participants something to do with their dogs year round. The dogs stay in better shape, keep tuned up on their marking, blinds, and general obedience, and arrive at the beginning of the hunting season in far better fettle than their counterparts who spend ten months of the year loafing. Retriever training benefits the dog owner as well, especially for those of us who find working with dogs an interesting activity. Small groups of enthusiasts can get together at regular intervals for training days, compare notes, and exchange bird throwing duties with one another.

Field Trials

Retriever field trials, now licensed by the American Kennel Club, are the oldest form of competitive sport for the retriever breeds. Labrador trials had their start in England, and continue there today much as they did in the early days. The emphasis in the British trials is on steadiness and manners, and the birds are mostly pheasants and grouse shot in typical British fashion — driven birds, flushed by beaters, toward a line of gunners. A small number of dog handlers stand in a line, sending their dogs for retrieves as designated by the judges.

The American trials trace their infancy to the late 1920s and were primarily an effort on the part of the Long Island gentry to duplicate retriever trials in the British manner — complete with imported British Labrador retrievers. At approximately the same time, while the Labradors of the well-to-do were retrieving upland birds in their trials, the Chesapeake Bay retriever folk were setting up competitions involving mostly waterfowl retrieves.

According to two trainers who were there from the beginning of the sport, the late Charles Kostrewski and the late Ray Staudinger, the Labrador people were envious of the water work being done by the Chesapeakes, and embarked on a program to excel in water work — as they did.

Retriever trials progressed rapidly from the early days, in which a blind retrieve could be completed successfully by throwing stones to attract a dog's attention to a bird he had not seen go down, to the present-day formula, which has been in practice at least since the mid-1940s. John attended trials with his father shortly after the end of WWII in which difficult blinds and multiple marks were standard in the Open All-Age stake. He was astounded to see a dog sent across a sizable body of water to be directed precisely to the location of a dead duck on the far shore with nothing more than a few whistles and hand signals. It was clear to John that such a dog was for him, having many times gone over his belt after a duck in the mucky quagmires of western Minnesota sloughs.

The regular stakes in a licensed trial include the Open All-Age (open to all dogs of the retrieving breeds), the Amateur All-Age (similar to the Open but handlers are required to be amateurs), and the Derby (for dogs under two years old). The last regular stake is the Qualifying, which is open to dogs who have not yet earned certain accomplishments.[1] Various non-regular stakes, such as puppy stakes, Hunters' Specials, and so forth were common at one time, but have become less so since the advent of hunt tests. Championship points toward the titles Field Champion (FC) and Amateur Field Champion (AFC) may be earned in the Open and Amateur stakes.[2] The Qualifying is similar in format to the Open and Amateur, but usually easier, with less competition. No championship points are awarded in the Qualifying, but a dog can become "Qualified All-Age" by placing first or second in a Qualifying stake, and many owners like

---

[1] Dogs are no longer eligible to run the Qualifying stake once they have either won two Qualifying stakes, obtained a place (first through fourth) or a JAM (Judges' Award of Merit) in an Open stake, or placed in an Amateur stake.

[2] The requirements for the Field Champion title are that a dog win at least one all-breed Open stake plus earn a total of at least 10 championship points, where five points are awarded for a win, three points for a second, one point for a third, and half a point for a fourth place. The title of Amateur Field Champion is awarded to a dog who earns these same accomplishments in the Open with an amateur handler, or earns fifteen points in the Amateur and Open stakes combined. Points earned in Limited, Special, or Restricted stakes count as Open points.

their dog's first trial experience to be at this, slightly easier level.[3]

Retriever field trials are intensely competitive. Most participants either pay professional trainers to train their dogs, often for the dogs' entire competitive lifetime, or dedicate much of their non-working time to training and to improving their training abilities. They make "pilgrimages" to visit successful trainers (amateur or pro), throwing birds and watching the trainers' techniques, and travel to seminars given by those accomplished in the sport. Puppies of the most sought-after breedings change hands for thousands of dollars at this writing. It is possible to be competitive without being rich — and the sport boasts a number of successful amateurs of modest means — but you will always have to compete against those who have put a lot of money into training, dogs, equipment, and high-class travel.

All stakes in field trials generally follow a fairly pat system of working from the less time-consuming land retrieves to the more difficult water blinds and finally the "piece de resistance," and more often for the contestants, the "coup de grace," — the final series water marks.

The Open, Amateur, and Qualifying have a standard format, beginning with a land triple or quad which is run by all contestants under conditions that are as uniform as possible. The dogs are run individually and must heel to the "line," the place from which they will be sent, usually a few feet in front of the two judges. When the dog is sitting in place, the handler usually lets the judges know with a hand signal that he or she is ready. The judges then signal the bird throwers, in prearranged order, to fire

---

[3]A dog can also become Qualified All-Age by getting a place or JAM (Judges' Award of Merit) in a licensed Open or Amateur stake. This status allows a dog to be entered in Limited and Special All-Age stakes, in which entrants are limited to Qualified dogs. The field-trial rules state that at least twelve Qualified All-Age dogs must be entered in a major stake (Open or Amateur) for it to carry championship points, but this is rarely an issue today, with hundred-dog trials commonplace.

their shotguns and throw their birds as close as possible to the same locations for all of the dogs.

These throwers are generally clothed in a white jacket so that the location from which the marks are thrown may be easily picked out by the dogs. Usually, a few seconds are allowed to pass between throws so that the dogs can concentrate on each mark individually. Usually, two of these marks are dead birds (pheasants or ducks) and one is a flier (live shot bird). Most frequently, the flier is the last bird down, but the judges may set a test in which it is thrown first or second — an "out of order" flier, which is more difficult.

After all of the marks have been thrown, the judges call the dog's number and the handler is free to send the dog for the marks in any order he or she wishes. While judges are forbidden to specify the order in which marks are picked up, they may require dogs to execute a blind retrieve before getting the marks. This test, called a "poison bird" blind because a dog that picks up a mark before getting the blind is dropped from the trial, is often the supreme test of control.

The second series is generally a land blind, and the third series is usually a water blind. On these blinds, handlers attempt to pick up the birds by lining (sending the dog in the general direction), and handling (blowing the whistle to stop the dog and casting it in a new direction, left, right, back, or come-in, by means of arm gestures as introduced in Chapter 9). The land and water blinds make use of various complications such as challenging terrain, cover, shoreline, poison birds, "dry shots" where no bird is thrown, tempting scented areas, and difficult wind conditions.

The land blind is often combined with the land marks as a single series, but the water blind is most often run as an isolated test for reasons of economy of time. Many consider the water blind to be the high point, and most difficult part of the sport. Our opinion is that the water marks are more often than not the "killer" that separates the winner and placements from the also-rans.

After each series is completed (all dogs have run), judges issue "callbacks," a list of the numbers of the dogs whose work was good enough to keep them in contention to win the trial. Only these dogs will compete in the next series. Because a field trial is competitive, a "passing grade" depends to a large extent on the overall quality of the dog work. A job that might be a failure in one trial could be one of the strongest performances in another. Notwithstanding, there are some performance faults that result in automatic failure, such as breaking (going before the dog's number is called on a mark), switching birds (setting a bird down to pick up another, or quitting the hunt for one bird to go pick up another), refusing to go when sent, or failing to deliver to hand. Other faults — such as handling on a mark, "popping" (looking back at the handler for help, especially on a mark), excessively large, rambling hunt indicating a poor mark, taking a poor line on a blind, refusing whistles or casts — will usually cause a dog to be dropped, unless the quality of work overall is very bad. The exception is that if most or all dogs handle on a mark in the final series, some of these dogs may be awarded places or even win if no dogs are able to pick up all of the birds without a handle.

The result of the continued elimination of dogs after each series is a paring down of the field of contestants, usually starting with 50-100 dogs, to ten or a dozen at the beginning of the fourth and final series. By this time, most of the dogs have been eliminated for accumulated minor and moderate faults. These dogs' performances lag so far behind the frontrunners that they have no chance of winning the trial.

In addition to being the epitome of retriever work, the water marks are usually time-consuming, so it works well to hold them last when the smallest number of dogs are still in contention. Water marks may be triple or quadruple, and in the advanced stakes (Open and Amateur) generally involve a "retired gun," a thrower who hides after executing his throw. Retired guns are usual in the first series land marks of these stakes, and are sometimes used in the Qualifying land or water marks as well. In principle, a well-trained dog could "line" to the area of each visible gun station and come up with all of the birds. While in practice, this is usually difficult, hiding one or more gunners places greater demands on the dogs' memory and marking ability.

The fourth series water marks are usually so difficult that only one or two of the participants do them without handling (resorting to hand signals). These are usually the two top dogs, so placements in field trials are most often fairly unequivocal.

The fourth regular stake in a licensed trial is the Derby, open to retrievers between the ages of six months and two years. This stake consists entirely of marked retrieves, almost always doubles. Although blind retrieves are not part of the stake, almost all contestants have been taught to handle as a preliminary to teaching them to go straight to their marks. "Derby Points" are won by placing first through fourth, and dogs who distinguish themselves in the Derby are generally considered to be precocious, highly trainable, and gifted markers.

Judging of field trials is inherently subjective, a fault in one dog's performance often being weighed against a different fault in another's work. A trial is judged more on the relative merit of the dogs' work than it is on a theoretical standard. The hard fact is that some trials are so difficult that nobody does very well, so the judges must evaluate a lot of mediocre dog work. Others are too easy, so the judges must "pencil out" dogs — get picky about minor details in order to determine callbacks, placements, and a winner. Setting tests which give good "separation"(allowing some dogs to clearly distinguish themselves on merit), is a challenge and many judges' ability to do so consistently is remarkable. The ideal trial is one in which the best dogs come to the top by executing good work on difficult tests with the rest falling by the wayside. On his or her day, the hero comes through in the fourth series water marks to kick the behind of the other ten contestants, and walks off in glory with a blue ribbon.

Despite the best efforts of the club, workers, judges, and contestants, all competitors are subject to the "breaks of the game." This phrase refers to the element of luck or misfortune that can prevent a dog from winning a trial. Variations in wind, light, scenting conditions, location of falls (especially fliers), visibility of throws, and disruptions such as flushed wild game, shots and whistles from another stake, barking dogs, etc. can all make one dog's job more difficult than that of another. The presumption is that over many trials, good and bad luck even out and, despite paying a large entry fee, traveling perhaps hundreds of miles and spending three days sitting around in unpleasant weather, contestants are expected to take their lumps in good grace — and in particular not to challenge the judges' decisions.

Hunt Tests
We use the term "hunt tests" to refer collectively to the AKC Hunting Tests for Retrievers, the NAHRA Hunting Retriever Field Tests, and the UKC/HRC Licensed Hunts.

Hunt tests were devised relatively recently to afford the grass roots hunting fraternity a chance to improve their retrievers' work through better training, and to establish the general requirements of a fully-trained hunting retriever. Ostensibly, these events fill a gap created by the overly-sophisticated field trial world in that realistic situations for typical hunting scenarios can be trained for. Field trials have clearly gone well beyond the limits of the average retriever owner and his or her dog. The commitment of time, talent, and dog quality is just too extreme.

According to our (John's) recollection, the hunt test idea was conceived by Richard Wolters (of writing fame), Jack Jagoda, and Ned Spear. The original plan was to establish a program under the auspices of the AKC. As things turned out, however, these three founded an autonomous organization devoted to retriever hunting tests, the North American Hunting Retriever Association (NAHRA), which commenced its "hunting retriever field tests" at about the same time that the AKC launched their own retriever hunting test program. Also at about that time, the United Kennel Club (UKC), the nation's second-largest and second-oldest dog registry, launched its Hunting Retriever Club (HRC) program. The avowed purpose of all three bodies was to make available standardized tests at multiple levels, to encourage the training of hunting retrievers, and to acknowledge and reward those who meet certain standards.

There is considerable similarity between the AKC and NAHRA programs. Each has three levels and evaluates dogs on many of the same traits emphasized in field trials: marking, memory, perseverance, courage, style or enthusiasm, and in the upper levels, more trained abilities including steadiness and blind retrieves. Each employs multiple marking tests in which throws are a few seconds apart, and all dogs are run on the same marks from the same starting line. As in AKC field trials, marking is considered the dog's responsibility and judges may not specify the order in which marks are retrieved. Hunt tests differ from field trials, however, in being explicitly noncompetitive. Dogs are judged against a set standard and trainers are encouraged to train to that standard. Callbacks are given after each series. Dogs with clearly failing work are dropped; dogs who still have a chance of obtaining an overall passing score are carried. Since the events are not competitive, the quality of other dogs' work is not supposed to affect whether a particular dog is called back or not.

We are less familiar with the UKC program. We have not yet attended one of their events, which have been few in our area until recently. Based on a reading of the rules and conversations with participants, the UKC Hunting Retriever Club testing program is somewhat different than those of AKC and NAHRA. Entries are limited and all dogs run all series, whether their work meets the standard or not. The number of dogs one handler may run is limited to eight, or fewer at the host club's discretion. We are told these events have a high proportion of owner/handlers, whereas the AKC and NAHRA hunt tests are often attended by professional trainers, each with a truckload of dogs. The title structure in the UKC program appears to be designed, more so than the other programs, to encourage participants to start at the simplest level and work their way upward.

The UKC encourages participants to register their dogs with UKC by giving UKC-registered dogs priority in the entry process, and awarding points and titles only to UKC-registered dogs. While some upland work may be included in UKC retriever tests, there is also an upland-only category leading to the title UH, or Upland Hunter.

In order to prevent the hunt tests escalating in difficulty as the competitive field trials have done, certain limits were imposed, which also allow judges considerable discretion to use the available grounds as they see fit. Limits to the length of retrieves — 100 yards or less in AKC events, shorter in the lower-level UKC and NAHRA tests — provide a limitation to the difficulty level. In addition, in keeping with the focus on identifying effective hunting dogs, a certain amount of handling on marks is permissible in hunt tests.

Other differences between AKC field trials and the hunt test programs are associated with the fact that a hunt test is designed as a simulated hunt, while a field trial is a test of retriever performance pure and simple. Handlers in hunt tests are required to wear dark or camouflage clothing, attiring themselves to look like hunters instead of dressing for maximum visibility on long blind retrieves. Throwers, too, are dressed in camo or hidden from view altogether, and shouts or game calls are sometimes used so he can attract a dog's attention to mark the falls. The NAHRA rules call for a shot to be fired when the bird is at the top of its arc, presumably to create the illusion that the bird is falling after being shot. In all programs, handlers are required to carry and, in the upper levels, shoulder an empty shotgun. In the UKC events, handlers fire poppers at thrown birds. Large decoy spreads and other accouterments of hunting are often realistically employed. "Wingers" (bird catapults) are commonly used to throw birds much farther than most bird boys can. Although wingers are used in some field trials, we have not seen them often.

The three hunt test programs include different groups of skills. AKC hunt test rules explicitly require only marked and blind retrieves, including "walk-up" and "diversion" marks, while the upper NAHRA classes include, and the UKC test may include, upland trailing and flushing tests. AKC directs that additional tests should be incorporated that are typical of hunting in the region where the test is held. The titles issued by UKC and NAHRA are prefix titles, placed before a dog's name, but the AKC has a strict policy that non-competitive titles must follow a dog's name, so the AKC hunt test titles are all suffix titles.

Levels of Difficulty

At the introductory level of all three programs (AKC Junior, NAHRA Started, UKC Started), only single marks are required, at least two on land and two from water. Dogs may be restrained with a slip cord until their number is called. In the AKC program, dogs must deliver to hand, while the other programs do not require delivery to hand. Retrieves are limited to 100 yards or less in the AKC Junior, 75 yards maximum in the others. The single marks at this distance can be challenging, however, and we recommend waiting to enter until a dog has been force-fetched and had a good deal of marking practice. Titles awarded after completion of the requisite number of events are Junior Hunter, or the letters JH placed after a dog's name (AKC) and Started Hunting Retriever, or the letters SR, placed before the dog's name (NAHRA).

In the middle level — AKC Senior, NAHRA Intermediate, or UKC Seasoned — double marked retrieves on land and on water are required. Simple land and water blinds are also required (water only in NAHRA). The falls that make up the double marks are generally more challenging than those in the Started/Junior levels, but usually the difficulty is in the use of decoys and natural features, not sophisticated "tight" or tricky tests. To do well, dogs need to have developed some proficiency and confidence at doubles marking, not be just beginning doubles. Dogs must be steady and deliver birds to hand.

A "walk-up," in which a bird is thrown while the handler walks with dog at heel, is required in the AKC Senior and permitted in the NAHRA and UKC events; the AKC Senior also includes an honor, where the dog sits steady as marks are thrown and another dog is sent for the retrieve. UKC Seasoned tests include a "diversion" (bulldog), but dogs are not failed for switching birds. Upland hunting tests, including trailing and/or quartering, are usual in the NAHRA Intermediate and UKC Seasoned. Live rounds are not fired over the dog in either event. Titles awarded are Senior Hunter, SH (AKC), Working

Retriever, WR (NAHRA), and Hunting Retriever, HR (UKC).

The next level leads to the "Master" titles: AKC Master Hunter (MH) or NAHRA Master Hunting Retriever (MHR). The top level NAHRA hunt tests, however, are referred to as the Senior division, so Senior has different implications in the two programs. The corresponding UKC level is Finished, leading to the Hunting Retriever Champion (HRCH) title. These events incorporate multiple marks, usually triples, and blind retrieves, with at least one blind generally run through a set of marks. Delayed marks, dry shots (shots fired with no bird thrown), diversions, and walk-ups are common or required. "Poison bird" blinds are often used. An honor is required in the AKC Master and may be included in the NAHRA Senior. A higher degree of polish is expected than in the preceding levels.

Distances to all retrieves at this level are limited to 100 yards or less except in UKC Finished, where marks may be 150 yards on land and 125 yards in water. UKC Finished also differs from the other two programs by allowing birds to be thrown with no shot or call to attract the dog's attention to the throwing location. To help direct their dogs' attention to the throw, some handlers teach their dogs to look in the direction of a pointed gun. The NAHRA Senior also includes a trailing test and an upland hunting test including the flush of a live bird, which may be shot or allowed to fly away. UKC Finished may include upland tests at the judges' discretion.

NAHRA offers a further title — GMHR, Grand Master Hunting Retriever — to dogs who pass a number of additional Senior tests.

UKC has an additional level: Grand. As with other UKC sporting-dog programs, the Grand level is only for dogs who have earned titles at the prior level, in this case the Finished level. Although Grand events, like the others, are noncompetitive, the language used to describe them suggests that title holders are the elite among hunting retrievers, and the tests are expected to be demanding. Distances up to 200 yards are used, and Grand tests incorporate a challenge unique among retriever events: judges may specify the order in which marks are to be retrieved. This "selection" employs different skills than the pure initiative and talent called for in the other events: either highly developed lining ability, or a memory for marks that is not overly disrupted by handler interference. Of course, the prescribed order may match a dog's natural preference, in which case he is likely to do well. The title earned at this level is GRHRCH — Grand Hunting Retriever Champion.

Because of the noncompetitive nature of hunting tests, the "breaks of the game" are not as heartbreaking as they are in field trials. There is, however, plenty that can happen to upset a dog and handler. In particular, there is ample room for differences in opinion as to what constitutes good, or even passing, dog work. Furthermore, sometimes the "mechanics" of the event go smoothly and everyone feels they are being treated well, but frequently there is a weak point somewhere. It is worthwhile to remember that the individuals putting on the event are volunteers, and that the efforts of a lot of people are needed to hold a hunting test; this almost always means some of them are inexperienced. As in field trials, good sportsmanship involves recognizing that others are subject to the same frustrations and disappointments—if not this week, then maybe next time.

Our descriptions of the various venues of retriever sport are intended to give you an idea of what to expect and are not a complete summary of what you need to know. We strongly recommend you write to the sponsoring organization for a copy of the rules and attend an event as a spectator (or volunteer) before entering.

Copies of the rules may be obtained from:

AKC Field Trials and Hunting Tests for Retrievers (1 copy free):
The American Kennel Club
5580 Centerview Drive
Suite 200
Raleigh, NC 27606-3390
www.akc.org
(be sure to specify retriever field trials or retriever hunting tests)

NAHRA Hunting Retriever Field Tests (1 copy free):
North American Hunting Retriever Association
P. O. Box 1590
Stafford, VA 22555
www.nahra.org

UKC-HRC Licensed Hunts (currently $4.50):
Hunting Retriever Championship Dept.
United Kennel Club Inc.
100 East Kilgore Rd
Kalamazoo, MI 49002-5584
www.hrc-ukc.com

WINNING

N OTHING BEATS WINNING. We must admit, however, that in the sport of field trialing retrievers, wins are infrequent enough to demand other rewards than blue ribbons. Even the greatest dogs, and the most consistent ones, do not win all the time, or even very close to it. A retriever that wins an Open or two every year, and qualifies for the National field trial is very good, and he or she will generally run 20-30 trials during the year to achieve this record. So the win is a golden moment — and a brief one.

The pinnacle of the sport in field trials occurs when you are running an excellent dog who somehow aces the most difficult tests of the trial, while other very good competitors fall apart on the same. Several years ago, FC-AFC Jaffers Blackie, a trainee of mine, was being handled by his owner for the first time in an Open All-Age stake. The day was windy with gusts over 50 mph and cold, in the forties, and nobody was doing well on the water blind. This test consisted of an angled entry into the water cross-ing a relatively calm 75-yard swim protected by the shore on the left and an island on the right. Once the dog broke into the windswept water beyond the point of the island, though, he had to negotiate a 100-yard swim across very rough water, bucking a mighty crosswind.

All of the dogs except Blackie were badly blown off course by this gale, but when he hit that stretch he held his line like a hove-to Gloucester schooner, and ended up on his objective with only a few casts and an excellent line. We could see a win in the making.

The next and final test consisted of a water triple in the opposite direction from the water blind. Three birds were thrown — one on a long narrow island to the left, and one on the near shore to the right. The big memory bird was between these two marks at a distance of about 175 yards and involved crossing about 75 yards of two-foot waves in a crosswind. The mark was a retired-gun duck some 50 yards up a hill in high cover on the far shore. Once again, Blackie's great drive in the water served him well. He crossed the initial, relatively calm water on line and entered the squall beyond headed directly toward the bird. He carried this line through some of the roughest water I have seen a dog retrieve in. His head was visible only briefly as it crested the waves. When Blackie reached the far shore, he headed up the hill at a run and scooped up his duck with a perfect mark.

These are the moments that are exciting, that remain forever imprinted in our memories. But the laurels belong not to the owner, nor the handler, but to the dog with the great heart, and the unquenchable desire to get his bird.

Blackie's career was cut short by health complications resulting from an injury early in life and he was forced into an early retirement. The remarkable things that he did in competition, in the hunting field, and as a family pet more than compensated for the relatively short duration of his life.

Right, nothing beats winning, and surely, nothing can match that first win. Jade (Tarheel Jade), the first retriever I trained mainly for field trial competition, provided me with that unforgettable experience by winning the largest Open All-Age stake I have entered — 105 dogs. The competition was stiff and included most of the top pros migrating North after their winter's training in the South. Great dogs in the prime of their lives, such as NAFC-FC Dee's Dandy Dude, his brother FC

Zipper Dee Do, and many other outstanding performers were my competition.

Large Opens (80 dogs and over) are generally set up very high on the difficulty scale so as to eliminate dogs quickly, thereby reducing the number of contestants to a workable level within the allotted time. This trial (Tarheel Retriever Club, Spring 1977, Weldon, NC) was a good example.

The combined first and second series involved a very difficult land triple with a retired gun and a blind. The attrition was so high from this test, which took all day Friday, that by Saturday morning the field was reduced to a normal size. Jade aced the marks and blind.

The third test was a water blind, not particularly difficult, composed of an angled entry down the shore of a stump pond about 100 yards in length. This test, while not a serious challenge to the good water dogs, took care of the residue from the first two series who disliked getting into cold water, further reducing the number of players. Once again, Jade did well, getting the blind on a good line with two or three corrective handles.

My hopes for success in the fourth, and most likely final series were crushed when I saw the layout the judges had set up: three down-the-shore, two thrown to the left and one to the right, all on the same strip of land and very tight (close together). The day was dark and cold, as March days often are and, though Jade had a great trial going up to this point, I was fully aware that this was not her test. I had, in fact, trained on it too much and too hard, and she only had to look at the gunners' positions in such a test to fall into a slump.

I approached the line with Jade with what I would conservatively call trepidation. It was by now darker and colder than ever. The sun had set, visibility was poor, and the test seemed impossible. No one had yet done it well.

Jade, surprisingly, came to the line with confidence, enthusiasm, and concentration. Bird number one went well, but the "money" bird was bird two, which was the shorter of the two ducks thrown to the left. Dog after dog had been sent for that fall, only to blow through the area of the mark and pick up the long bird. In some cases this was graded a switch and out (switching birds is an automatic failure in a field trial), and in others merely a bad line to the mark if the dog did not hunt the area of the shorter fall.

Jade, however, nailed the shorter of the two birds thrown to the left, came back, and pinned the long mark to score a perfect triple. This performance met with general approbation from the judges and gallery, but I detected some grapes of the not-so-sweet variety from contestants with top dogs who had failed or messed up the test.

That night, it was a glorious evening at the start with a wonderful cocktail party and hors d'oeuvres, and the rumor rife that Jade had won the trial. Even the field-trial chairman confided that I had won and the trial was over. Then the roof fell in when an unexpected announcement came over the rumble of the cocktailers on the bullhorn, "Fifth series in the Open tomorrow morning at eight. The judges do not have a clear winner!"

By this time, paranoia had set in — 105 dogs, impossible tests, water marks that were definitely not Jade's bag — and now a fifth series because the judges did not have a "clear winner." I had come from out of nowhere with my titleless bitch to threaten all the greats of the time with a win over many of the country's best retrievers. It has occurred to me often that this just didn't seem right to the judges — not the way things ought to go.

So, up and at 'em at 8 o'clock Sunday morning. There were ten dogs or so left in the trial, most of them nicked here or there by a weak series with the exception of Jade, who was, as we say, "clean."

I was running in rotation, a way of numerically staggering the running order of dogs so the same one doesn't go first all the time, and faced a very tough test on a backwards L-shaped piece of water. The line of departure was about 75 yards from the base of the L. The first retrieve was a duck thrown midway across the base of the L and into the cattails on the far side. The second retrieve was a blind up the channel of the long leg of the L and 50 yards beyond the water in the field. I had confidence here because Jade was a wonderful water blind dog. She pinned her marked duck, returned and lined all the way to the end of the channel, needing only one cast to kick her out of the water at the end and carry her to her objective. It was a near-perfect performance. Nothing could take the win from her now.

Strangely, the exhilaration of that win was not quite what I expected. The intensity of joy was greatest while anticipating the tests, and then doing them flawlessly. Anticipation, expectations, training, and rolling with the punches when the breaks go against you — that's what makes competition.

What is a win? Maybe it's not the five points, or the title, or your name in *Field Trial News*, or the public approval, brief as it is. It just might be the memory of a great dog, and the work you put into building the partnership necessary to make a winning team.

APPENDIX

GLOSSARY OF TERMS

Amateur: In field trials, anyone who is not a pro, i.e. does not take money to train or handle a dog. Only amateurs may judge or run the Amateur All-Age stake.

Angle back: Cast given with the arm at an angle between straight out and straight up, with or without a verbal "Back!" The dog translates the gesture into an angle between straight over and straight back. The direction taken by the dog may or may not be literal (the exact angle of the handler's arm from vertical).

Attitude: Dog's general predisposition to work.

Attrition: An approach to correcting a dog's behavior that is particularly useful in the teaching of blind retrieves. Forceful corrections (with the electric collar, for example) are kept to a minimum. Instead, the dog is stopped every time he makes or repeats an error, and the desired command or cast is repeated until finally the dog complies.

Back (direction): Straight out in the direction the handler is faced.

Back (command): Send command used by most trainers on blind retrieves and by some trainers on all retrieves.

Back (cast): Given with one arm raised straight up, with or without a verbal "Back!". This cast orders the dog to turn and run straight away from the handler.

Bird: Sometimes used to mean the object retrieved, whether bird or dummy, as in "bird thrower," or "memory bird."

Blind retrieve: A retrieve in which the dog does not see a bird fall, or forgets the location of a bird it has seen. The handler directs the dog to the bird by means of whistle, voice, and hand signals.

Blind: In hunting, a hide for the hunter and/or dog. In events, usually a three-sided screen behind which a handler and dog wait to run so that the dog cannot see the marks thrown for other dogs. A retiring blind is a similar construction, used by throwers to hide after throwing a bird.

Break: When the dog leaves on a retrieve without being sent.

Bulldog: Mark thrown while a dog is returning with another mark. The dog is supposed to hold on to the bird he is carrying (as a bulldog holds on) and not switch to the other thrown bird.

Bumper: A retrieving dummy — similar to a small boat bumper.

Cast: A hand and arm signal used to give a direction to a dog.

Cheat: To avoid water or another obstacle by running around it. Cheating is undesirable because it typically leads to poor marking, and may lead to extreme avoidance of obstacles and refusal to retrieve.

Collar: Sometimes used to refer specifically to the electric collar, as in "collar-trained dog."

Creeping: Motion by the dog on the line short of breaking. Once established, this behavior can be difficult to control.

Diversion (traditional): A short mark that is retrieved before a longer memory bird or blind retrieve; the short mark diverts the dog's attention from the memory bird or blind retrieve.

Diversion (in hunting tests): Traditionally known as a "bulldog," it is a mark thrown while the dog is going to or, usually, returning from another mark. The dog is required to hold on to the bird in his mouth (like a bulldog) and not "switch" birds.

Double Marked Retrieve or **Double:** Actually two retrieves. The dog watches both birds or dummies fall, retrieves the first to hand, then goes to retrieve the other. The second bird is referred to as a "memory bird" since the dog must remember it while retrieving the first one.

Draw: Order of running dogs in an event.

Dry shot: A shot which is not accompanied by a thrown bird or dummy.

Dummy: Object thrown or placed for a dog to retrieve. Usually plastic or canvas-covered. Also called a bumper.

flier: Live bird thrown into the air and shot for the dog to retrieve. The excitement of a live bird is a training issue. If not specified as a flier, a thrown bird is assumed to be dead.

flyaway: Live bird that is missed by the gunners and flies away. This makes marking and retrieving a second bird, thrown and shot from the same station, more difficult than it would otherwise be. When it happens in a trial, it puts a dog at a disadvantage. See "No bird."

Force-fetch or **force break:** The process of training a dog to retrieve as a matter of obedience, not of play. It usually brings about a general improvement in a dog's work, including greater enthusiasm; it also prevents mouth problems, and makes retrieving reliable.

Force on back: The process of teaching a dog that it must go when sent; retrieving is not optional.

Freebie or **happy bumper:** A dummy thrown by hand purely as a reward or relaxation for the dog. Usually the dog is allowed to break.

Freezing: Situation where a dog returns with a bird but does not give it up to the handler. Also called "sticking."

Guns: Shooters (throwers) in the field.

Handle: To stop a dog with a whistle and give it a cast; or to heel a dog to the line and run it on one or more retrieves.

Handling: Directing a dog to a fall by means of whistle, voice, and hand signals. A "handling dog" is one that has been trained to obey these signals.

Hard dog: A dog of unusually tough nature in its response to correction.

Hard mouth: Usually describes a dog that habitually bites down on a bird it is carrying, causing damage to the bird. In events, crushed bone structure is the usual criterion for identifying a hard-mouthed dog. Also used for a dog who eats birds instead of delivering them.

Honest: Said of a dog who goes straight to its objective through any water, cover changes, or other obstacles that may be en route. Honesty is desirable because it leads to better marking than the alternative of cheating, or running around.

Honor (verb): For a dog to sit quietly as marks are thrown and another dog is sent to retrieve them. (Noun) A test, in a field trial or hunt test, where dogs are required to honor. A "cold honor" is a test where the dog honors prior to retrieving any birds.

Hunt (verb): To search for a bird or dummy.

Hunt (noun): A dog's efforts to search up a bird it has marked but does not instantly find. In competition, giving up the hunt is grounds for failing a dog. A good, determined, intelligent hunt is an important asset in a working retriever, since it is presumed that birds may move, drift, or be impossible to pinpoint.

Indirect pressure: A method of correction that is useful during advanced or potentially-confusing retrieving work. Instead of being corrected at the moment of infraction, the dog is brought under control (usually by making him sit), then given a correction, usually with the electric collar. This approach avoids the problem of the dog's associating the correction with some desirable aspect of its behavior.

JAM: Judges' Award of Merit, also known as a "green" since the award is a green ribbon. Awarded at the end of a field trial to dogs whose work throughout is good but who do not place first through fourth.

Line: Direction the handler gives the dog on a blind retrieve.

Line (sending): The location from which the handler sends the dog for a bird, in training or in an event.

Line (verb): Said of a dog; to go out in the direction given by the handler.

Line the blind: To execute a blind retrieve on a good initial line, with no handles.

Mark or **Marked retrieve**: A retrieve in which the dog sees the dummy or bird fall and finds it without help from the handler

Marking: The skill of locating a fallen bird or dummy, accurately navigating the intervening terrain, cover, or water. While marking effectiveness can be improved by training dogs to run straight and practicing certain layouts, the ability is largely inherited.

Memory bird: A bird or dummy in a multiple mark that the dog retrieves after retrieving, or watching, another thrown bird or dummy. Normally, the last bird or dummy thrown is the shortest (the diversion) and the dog picks this up first — then the remaining falls are memory birds. On an out-of-order setup, many dogs do not retrieve the last bird first, and all of the throws are considered memory birds.

Momentum: Characteristic of a dog with great range and sustained purposefulness.

Multiple mark or **Multiple fall**: Retrieving situation where a dog watches more than one bird or dummy fall, then goes to get them one at a time.

National: The National Open Retriever Championship, held once a year, one stake for all of the eligible retriever breeds. May also refer to the National Amateur stake and to the Canadian National Open and Amateur stakes.

Nick: To administer shock with the e-collar.

No bird: Situation where a bird is thrown or shot in a way that makes the mark more, or less, difficult than intended, and a decision is made not to run the dog on the test. Examples: a flier might be shot too close or in the wrong direction; a bird intended to fall on land might fall in the water; the throw might be too low to be clearly visible. All birds are picked up and re-thrown. In an event, usually a no bird puts a dog at a disadvantage, so judges must decide whether it is worse to run the bad bird or to come back and try again. "No bird" is also a cue given by the handler when the dog is not to retrieve, as in an honor.

No-go: When a dog is commanded to retrieve but does not.

Old fall: Fall area in which a dog has already picked up the bird. Returning to hunt an old fall is an automatic failure in a field trial, unless marks are so close together that the areas overlap.

Out-of-order: A multiple retrieve in which the last bird or dummy down is farther away than one of the others. It is much easier for an inexperienced dog to pick up the last bird to fall if it is also the shortest, in which case a dog will almost always pick it up first. An out-of-order double or triple provides a number of ways for a dog to fail. It is confusing to inexperienced dogs, and most dogs can do such tests reliably only with specific training. A test is also considered out-of-order, and difficult, if the flier is not the last bird down.

Over: Cast given to one side or the other, with arm extended in the desired direction. When the dog is far away, an over may be emphasized by taking a couple of steps in the direction indicated.

Over and Under: Marks thrown "in line" so that the dog runs through the area of the shorter mark on its way to the longer one.

Pattern: Drill involving piles of dummies in various formations: T, double T, etc.

Pin: To get a mark "from the front" with no hunt — a perfect job.

Plug: A slow-moving, unstylish dog. May be due to overly-harsh training, a lack of confidence, or a lack of interest inherent in the dog. Also "pig."

Poison bird: A retrieving test in which one or more marks are thrown (or shot) but the dog is required to pick up a blind retrieve (or more than one) before getting the mark(s). If a dog gets a mark before doing the blind, it fails the test.

Pop: To look back at the handler for help on a retrieve when the handler has not blown his or her whistle. Considered a fault. Avoiding the creation of a popping problem is one of the guiding principles behind modern training methods.

Pro: Anyone who takes money to train someone else's dog.

Pressure: Used for the physical force applied in training, and also to the overall stress of training.

Puppy Stake: Competition for dogs under one year or other age criterion i.e. six months, nine months, etc.

Retired gun: A thrower (gun) who hides, either by sitting down behind a blind or by moving to a hiding place, after the bird is thrown and before the dog picks up the mark.

Scrap a test: Give up on a test and substitute another. In a field trial, this can only be done before all dogs have completed a test.

Scratch: Withdraw a dog from an event. Most often used for bitches in season or injured dogs.

Soft: Said of a dog who does not learn effectively from heavy training pressure.

Started: Said of a dog who has had some training in retrieving, but has not yet learned to handle.

Style: The appearance of enthusiasm, enjoyment, and confidence in a dog's work. While not all stylish dogs are extremely fast, they show eagerness to get to their bird or dummy and do not dawdle or shirk.

Switch: To leave the area of a marked fall after establishing a hunt but without finding the bird to go retrieve a different bird. Less often, to set down a bird and pick up another.

Test: General term used for training setups in the field, involving marks and/or blinds, as well as similar setups used in competition.

Tight: Said of the throws in a multiple mark if there is a small angle between the lines to the different falls. After picking up the shorter of the marks, a dog must run close by that same spot on the way to the longer mark. This can be very confusing to an inexperienced dog.

APPROXIMATE TIMETABLE FOR RETRIEVER TRAINING

LMOST EVERYONE UNDERTAKING TO TRAIN his or her dog wants to know how long it will take, and specifically, how much time is required for certain procedures. It can be very useful to have a guide that helps determine whether you are getting bogged down or perhaps pushing your dog too fast, and it's nice to have some idea, months ahead of time, whether your work with your dog can be expected to have him or her well-prepared for hunting season. The problem with predicting time requirements is that there are many sources of variability. Dogs mature at different rates and learn at different rates — and many of them have a hang-up somewhere along the line where a training procedure takes longer than it does with most dogs. Novice trainers have differing abilities to communicate with their dogs, and different degrees of dedication to regular work and to rigorous consistency. We caution you to use the information presented on the following page as a general guide only — and in particular, not to give it more credence than your own judgment of when your dog is proficient at one level and ready to move on.

Topic	Age to Begin	Other Indication of Readiness to Begin	Time Required
Puppy retrieves	As soon as you get your puppy		
Marking		Your pup must do an orderly retrieve; this may be only after force fetching	lifelong
Introduction to birds	Before 6 months		one or a few sessions
Introduction to water		As early as possible; water must be above 56°	
Basic obedience (sit, heel, stay, here)	After 4 months (sit may be taught sooner)		Practice, gently, until age 6 months
Reliable off-lead obedience	After 6 months		
Force fetch (from "hold" through walking stick fetch)	After 6 months	Dog must "sit" promptly and come reliably on a single command	Usually 1-2 months; may be a few days or 3 months
Steadying	Don't rush this; continue with slip cord until over 12 months	Usually after force fetching is complete	lifelong
Yard pattern (forcing to pile and casts)	7-10 months or later	After force fetching is complete and steadying is begun	Usually 1-2 months, but may take much longer
School blinds	8-12 months or later	After yard pattern is completed	lifelong
Cold blinds	9-12 months and on	Introduced after school blinds are established	lifelong

INDEX